THE THIRD WORLD:
NEW DIRECTIONS

THE THIRD WORLD: NEW DIRECTIONS

Q————————————————

ZULFIKAR ALI BHUTTO
Prime Minister of Pakistan

QUARTET BOOKS · LONDON

First published by
Quartet Books Limited 1977
A member of the Namara Group
27 Goodge Street, London W1P 1FD

Copyright © 1977 by Zulfikar Ali Bhutto

ISBN 0 7043 2145 9

Typesetting by Bedford Typesetters Limited, Bedford
Printed by Anchor Press, Tiptree, Essex
Bound by Mansell (Bookbinders) Limited, Witham, Essex

Acknowledgement

We wish to thank the *Spectator* for permission to reprint an interview by George Hutchinson with Mr Bhutto (September 1976), Copyright © the *Spectator*.

Other books by the author:

The Myth of Independence
Peace-Keeping by the United Nations
The Great Tragedy
Politics of the People (3 vols.)

CONTENTS

Foreword   13
The Imperative of Unity   17
Bilateralism   31
Regional Cooperation for Development   61
The Role of the Muslim States   75
Pakistan and the World   95

Notes on Bilateralism   105
Index   133

THE THIRD WORLD:
NEW DIRECTIONS

FOREWORD

The cares of office are not the least of ills
that flesh is heir to. While this may be true in any age or
clime, it gains an added pertinence in a developing country
in the last quarter of the twentieth century. Myriad problems
besiege the head of government. Ranging from a person in
distress, a road in disrepair, a factory fallen into disuse, a
plan gone awry, an unprovided-for visitation of flood or
drought to the continuous issue of adjustment and readjustment
to a rapidly changing international environment, they demand
quick solutions and urgent remedies. Little time is left for
the kind of quiet thinking that would enable one to move
from the *ad hoc* to the conceptual plane. Theories abound,
of course. But more often than not, they appear to lack relation
with the concrete circumstances that one is compelled to
confront. I suppose that, if there were a social club of all
heads of government, especially of the Third World, the
narration of the experiences of one would be promptly echoed
by another and none would feel the slightest tedium.

My own experience, first as President of Pakistan from
December 1971 to August 1973 and as Prime Minister since,

has been especially onerous. I started with a broken country and a baffled people. The task of reconstruction was greatly complicated by a unique upheaval in the world economy. How to moderate its impact is a question which has occupied countless hours and days of anxious discussion.

If, despite these consuming preoccupations, I have taken time out to write the articles in this volume, it is because I feel that, unless a developing country formulates the principles, and works out the ethic, which should govern its responses to the external challenges of today and tomorrow, it runs a twofold risk. The lesser one is of being misunderstood by others. The greater one is that the executants of its own policies might lack a sense of direction, and therefore, be unable to summon that sense of commitment which is a prerequisite for their success.

I do not presume to speak for the entire Third World. Each country views matters in its individual geo-political setting. Each finds its own equilibrium. Each defines its own approach. But I cannot imagine that the conclusions which crystallize from my own, and Pakistan's, experience can lack relevance for other developing countries and for those who have to deal with them. While the domestic situations of the Third World countries may differ in varying degrees, their relationships *inter se* and with the developed countries, particularly with the great powers, pose questions of an identical pattern which need to be answered with confidence and conviction, if not with finality. On these answers depend the directions which the policies of governments in the Third World are going to take in the fateful years that lie ahead.

Z.A.B.

Rawalpindi
15 December, 1976

The pious declarations of the Sixth Special Session of the UN General Assembly and the Group of 77 having failed to bridge the gulf between the rich industrialized States and the poor dispossessed nations of the Third World, Pakistan's Prime Minister Bhutto appealed, during his visit to Pyongyang in May 1976, for a conference of the developing countries of Asia, Africa and Latin America to reach a consensus on the means to rectify the imbalance in the world economic order.

Explaining the rationale of such a conference, Bhutto wrote this article on the eve of the Mexico Conference held in September 1976, a month after the Summit Conference of the Non-aligned Countries and when the Paris Conference had reached a stalemate.

THE IMPERATIVE OF UNITY

The primal issue in human affairs on the international plane today is the division between the poor and the rich. There are hewers of wood and drawers of water, on the one side, and those who wield mastery over the planet's resources, on the other. The reality of this division, sometimes described as the North-South polarization, has been sharpened by the developments of the last three years.

The division need not amount to an unbridgeable gulf. A unique historical situation of which we are witnesses calls for nothing else but a creative dialogue between the two classes of nations. It demands the translation into international terms of the same process of building equitable economic orders and resolving class conflicts in which the leadership of many nations, north or south, east or west, is currently engaged in their domestic spheres.

Despite manifold appearances to the contrary, the dialogue is yet to be initiated in the manner and the kind of forum which can lead to a definite conclusion. It has been confused and fragmented. Soaked in a welter of formulations, it stands in danger of being smothered in verbiage. Worse still, it can be made a pawn in power politics, a base for manoeuvres or a cover for making arrangements which may not be ignoble in themselves but which distort the centrality of the historic issue.

What are the reasons for the confusion of the dialogue? To bring them into focus is not to deny the merit of the prodigious work done under the aegis of the Group of Seventy Seven which is reflected in the Algiers Charter, the Lima Declaration and Action Programme, the Dakar decisions and the Manila Declaration. Nor does it detract from the value of the resolutions on economic issues adopted by the non-aligned countries in Cairo, Georgetown, Algiers, Lima and, most recently, in Colombo. Least of all does it connote any disinterest in the kind of debate on a new economic order which was initiated at the Sixth Special Session of the United Nations General Assembly and which made some progress at the Seventh Special Session. It is clear, however, that all this effort has built only the infrastructure of thought for lending that new dimension of justice to international economic relations which alone can constitute an adequate response to humanity's present challenge.

Why this dimension of justice is not yet a reality is because there has yet been no organized movement for it from the Third World. The demonstrations of solidarity, made by the developing countries at international forums under the aegis of the United Nations, are no doubt sincere and deeply felt. Yet we cannot lull ourselves into the belief that the energies of the Third World are thereby focussed on the principal issue facing it today. The fissiparous condition of the Third World is apparent from the fact that all existing groupings of developing countries are based on the regional or political affiliations of their members and, being so self-limited, cannot address themselves to the issue which encompasses all regions and transcends differences of political or ideological orientation. Associations like the Islamic Conference, the Arab League, the Organization of African Unity and the economic organizations of Latin American countries, by virtue of their restrictive charters are confined to countries of a certain continent, region or faith. They do not, therefore, claim to comprehend the entirety of the economic interests of the developing countries.

Nor is such a claim advanced by the Group of Non-Aligned Countries. Though this Group has now enlarged itself to more than eighty members, it still excludes a large number of developing countries. A principle of composition which was linked to great-power relations at the time of the Group's genesis cannot bear an organic relation to the basic objectives and struggle of the Third World today. Leaving aside the fact that, contrary to the inclination of most non-aligned countries, the principle has been invidiously applied over the years, it is apparent that a division between one group of developing countries and the other can serve only to splinter the collective strength of the Third World. Both groups consist of countries which have suffered from imperialist or neo-colonial domination and are equal partners in the struggle to end international economic iniquities. I am happy that this reality has been powerfully articulated at the recent Colombo Conference. My esteemed friend, the Prime Minister of Sri Lanka, gave an authoritative utterance to the feeling of the majority of non-aligned states when she said that the non-aligned movement was not 'an exclusive club' and that the exclusiveness, if any, was that of the underprivileged. She added, 'It is not the non-aligned nations alone who have realized the potential for change. The entire Third World is now engaged in the process of organizing its political and economic strength to change old patterns of dependence and exploitation.' There could not be a better acknowledgement of the need to establish a wider basis for common action by all the deprived nations.

2

For a certain period, the necessity of the unity of developing countries was blurred by the appearance of a rapid re-alignment of economic power and influence in the world. The assertion by the oil-producing countries of their right to control their basic and depleting resource and to determine its price caught the imagination of suffering humanity as the dramatic correction of an age-old wrong. This gave rise to the hope that the older dispensation in which the principal resources of a group of countries were controlled, cheaply bought and extravagantly used for the growth and luxury of the richer countries would give way to a new order in which these resources would be used for the benefit of their rightful owners. That these hopes have languished is an indubitable fact. But the development itself relating to the price of one commodity, oil, demonstrated the effect that can be achieved by a unity of purpose and the exertion of the political and economic will of the producing countries. It showed that long-standing institutions crumble, and conventional economic practices wither, when nations unite for their common benefit at turning-points in history.

The corollary is that when nations are divided, when they cannot forge a unity of purpose, they continue to suffer not only existing iniquities but also their aggravation through the workings of global economic forces. For the newly-independent countries of the Third World, the international economic environment was hostile even when they attained sovereign statehood. But, during the decades of their political independence, the economic inequality between them and the affluent countries has grown immeasurably. The result is that, in real terms, they are today behind even their starting point for economic and social development. Not to speak of the famine which took a tragic toll in recent years in parts of Africa, the hunger which stalks other lands, the chronic deficits in balance-of-payments and worsening terms of trade are but some indications of their plight. When a group from among them strives to end these iniquities, the massive economic power of the affluent countries asserts itself and the inherent bias of the institutions of trade and capital in their favour enables these countries to shift the weight of internal and external adjustments to the poorer nations. When the price of oil increased, the developed countries as a whole, made little or no sacrifice; they raised the prices of their industrial products and thus shifted the burden of the so-called oil crisis back to the Third World. When it comes to the primary products exported by the Third World, the developed countries again determine the prices because they are the main markets and disagreement on production quotas and other causes inhibit the developing countries from exerting their weight. This process cannot be arrested unless all the developing countries coordinate their objectives and act in unison. In the last decade and a half, the prices of primary commodities, with the exception of oil, which constitute the bulk of the Third World exports, have deteriorated by a substantial percentage in real terms. Added to this is the phenomenon of violent year-to-year fluctuations in the prices of these exports depending largely on economic activity in the affluent countries. When some developing countries acquire a manufacturing capacity and can sell manufactured goods, their products are excluded from the markets of the rich by restrictive quotas. All these factors lead to several consequences. The uncertainty about the prices of primary commodities turns the economic planning of the poorer countries to a gamble. The position regarding their manufactures thwarts their aim of achieving self-sufficiency. The necessity of having to pay more and more for the same imports from the richer countries sinks many among them deeper into the mire of debt. This is a pattern which repeats itself inexorably in the daily economic exchange in commodities, manufactures, technology and finance between the developed and the developing countries. Its cumulative result is almost total dependence.

In the face of all this, the thesis is being increasingly propagated that the growth and development of the poor must depend upon the continued rapid growth of the rich; for only then can the markets for the goods of the poor expand and the prices of their commodities hold. This is a pernicious doctrine. It means that the gap between the poor and the rich must continue to expand. It means that the rich must continue to appropriate an overwhelming proportion of the earth's wealth. It means that if, because of sheer saturation with goods, the rich should choose to grow less rapidly, there is no hope for the poor. But the irony is that, while we may justly denounce this doctrine, it merely describes an in-built feature of the present international economic order. It reflects the undeniable fact that our terms of trade, our markets and our resource flows are overwhelmingly dependent upon economic and political policies in the richer countries. While the fundamental under-pinnings of this system may not be changed overnight, there is an urgent need to provide the poorer countries an insurance against disaster. The future of the less privileged cannot be allowed to depend upon growing inequality. A way has to be found to improve the terms of trade for the Third World, to remove the iniquities of quotas and trade restrictions in the affluent countries and to reduce the paralysing burden of external debt which is largely a result of unequal trade and exchange between the poor and the rich.

3

We, the countries of the Third World, are called upon to squeeze centuries into decades. Not for us is the relaxed stance of countries which built their economies in an earlier and more tranquil age, which had to dismantle no institutions and which could be content with gradual reform and the steady workings of social change. We are trying to create an environment of opportunity, an ethos of dignity and hope for the under-privileged majority of our peoples. We cheerfully undertake the toil and sweat for a better life for our masses. We accept the denial of immediate comforts. But we cannot allow the value of our sacrifice to be jeopardized by institutions and practices which structurally operate against us. The labour of our masses is constantly being devalued by unequal economic relationships between us and the richer countries. We live on a thin margin. The radical changes in our societies that are inescapable for us permit little room for manoeuvre. The crisis of the mid-seventies, which originated in the developed countries, had its worst impact on us and retarded our development for many years. In a large number of Asian, African and Latin American countries, per capita income has declined. Some, like Pakistan, may have maintained and even accelerated the momentum of their development effort but this has inevitably resulted in greater indebtedness. In order to ensure self-generating growth, we all need to examine and review the external economic environment, and its integral link with our collective weaknesses, so that the global economy ceases to act like a strong current setting us back in our voyage to self-realization.

4

While all these elemental truths have been uttered at countless forums, the ironical fact remains that, instead of evoking the natural response of a sense of interdependence, they have caused the opposite reaction. This is visible in the growing self-righteousness among the rich. Poverty among nations is regarded as the result of inherent defects in peoples; one hears more and more the assertion that the less developed have none but themselves to blame for their plight. The rich are strengthening their groupings and associations and focussing their attention on the consolidation of their own gains. Thus issues of international monetary reform, trade and resource flows are largely settled amongst themselves and the influence of the developing countries is at best peripheral.

It is wholly unrealistic to expect from existing international institutions the capacity to rectify this imbalance. Those concerned with aid and monetary affairs have fallen prey to a re-

gressive trend among the rich and the powerful. The proportion
of external assistance to gross national product in the leading
nations among them has been steadily declining. Organizations
like the International Development Association and the United
Nations Development Programme suffer from paucity of funds.
Perennial negotiations on trade have failed to eliminate the
restrictions of quotas on the exports of developing countries.
Textual battles are being fought on the issue of stabilizing and
improving the prices of raw material exports of developing
countries. Anodynes are administered in the form of resolutions.
The Paris Conference as anticipated faces a pathetic stalemate.
Operating at the level that they do, such institutions cannot
possibly rise to the height of the present challenge. A tepid
conversation cannot betoken a creative dialogue.

5

We are told that the countries of the Third World do not have
common interests regarding all the subjects at issue in the international economic order. There is said to be a discordance
between those who are concerned exclusively with the issue of
commodities and those who are semi-industrialized. Likewise,
it is asserted that the issue of debt relief is not important for
countries which have direct access to capital markets and are
interested in maintaining their 'creditworthiness'. But the
common interest of all the developing countries of Asia, Africa
and Latin America – the achievement of a position of equality
in the world economic order – far overrides any sectional
divergence. A complete identity of interest on each and every
issue is not the inescapable essential for unity. Difference is not
opposition. To give an example, the economic unity of the
Common Market, sustained by a network of institutions and
generating a common political purpose, is a more striking
phenomenon than any disparities between its member countries.
Unity is nurtured by mutual accommodation. It is born out

of the realization that, in its absence, everyone's interest will inevitably suffer.

6

We in the Third World are united by our common suffering and our common struggle against exploitation. Regardless of our political systems or our external outlook, we have the common mandate to extricate the world's majority from a throttling economic order. We need to develop a personality of our own. Let not this personality be torn by the schizo-phrenia which is caused by the failure to reconcile short-term interests with long-term goals. Let it not be confused by our inability to review the scope and area of mutual cooperation for our economic and social development. Let it not be en-feebled by the lack of the political will to exert our combined strength for changing a system that patently discriminates against the developing countries.

This political will cannot find expression except at the highest level of our collective leadership. Though the Third World has the vehicle of the Group of Seventy Seven to co-ordinate its common endeavours, the fact cannot be overlooked that the Group was created within the context of the Trade and Development Organization. Its perspective is, at times, limited by its origins and its mechanisms are too cumbersome to respond adequately to the imperatives of change. A restrictive organization which cannot articulate the political urge and the supreme authority of the developing countries can hardly be entrusted with the task of guiding their strategy.

There exists a growing awareness in the Third World of its latent strength. The consciousness is unmistakable that the most significant issue of our times is the opening of opportunity to the majority of the human race. On this issue there is no division between the so-called aligned and the so-called non-aligned; there exists only the difference between the developed and the underdeveloped. To underline this difference is not to call for a global class war. It is to call for that redistribution of economic power which alone can prevent unceasing strife and recurrent upheavals. It is to plead for the survival of the global community.

We do not harbour the illusion that the objective of a new and just economic order can be achieved through a single meeting or conference. The path to the economic independence of the Third World will be tortuous. But it can be made easier if the leadership of the Third World, backed by the power of human opinion, is united and resolute. For this purpose, I have issued an appeal for convening a conference of the developing countries of Asia, Africa and Latin America at the summit level in order to mobilize the full force of the peoples of the Third World behind their common struggle for liberation from international economic exploitation and oppression.

This appeal corresponds directly to a growing recognition of the imperative of the Third World's unity. Last month, the Summit Conference of the Non-Aligned Countries met in Colombo and addressed itself to this supreme issue of our times. Next week, representatives of the developing countries will meet at ministerial level in Mexico to consider ways and means of promoting economic cooperation among these countries. I am confident that the Mexico Conference will be another milestone along this path. The General Assembly of the United Nations is also going to meet later this month. The appropriate time has therefore arrived for Pakistan to set forth the basic considerations behind the call for the Third World Summit which will decisively consolidate the unity of the under-privileged majority of mankind.

Pakistan asks for cooperation from all developing countries in convening this conference and making its deliberations fruitful. It is more than two decades ago that the newly-independent countries met in Bandung and set out the political principles and purposes which would guide their international conduct. The Bandung Conference belied the fears that it would exacerbate the world political situation. Indeed, its declarations constitute a basic text for peaceful international relations. Likewise, the Third World Summit will be a significant step in an evolutionary process. It will mark the reaching of the next stage after policitcal liberation of the peoples of Asia, Africa and Latin America: the one at which an equality of opportunity for the world's peoples does not depend on charity through larger foreign assistance or piecemeal reform through selective trade concessions and the like. It will signal the turning away from the threat of a simmering and potentially disastrous confrontation to the promise of a global partnership. In the ultimate analysis the generation of economic activity in the developing countries is an essential for the well-being of the developed countries as well. The Summit of the poor will demonstrate their resolve not to wait passively for this realization in the industrialized economies.

By taking stock of the situation, devising a strategy for the future and making appropriate institutional arrangements, the Third World Summit can co-ordinate the policies and reconcile the positions of the Third World countries vis-a-vis the developed countries and evolve and implement an agreed minimum programme of cooperation among the developing countries. It will thus bring together and harmonize the efforts launched in several groupings of developing countries, regional or inter-regional, and enable the Third World to emerge stronger and take its rightful place in the world economic community.

The Third World's message must not be clothed in the jargon of a bygone age nor be tailored to the political ends of any country or group of countries. If the opulent and the powerful can combine, as they invariably do at critical moments, to maintain their dominance on the basis of their wealth and technology, it would be perpetrating a wrong on humanity if the poor nations should dissipate their relatively limited strength in dividing their own ranks, in creating a gulf between the poor and the poor. The impoverished masses of the Third World are yearning for a new focal point of their collective will. They are seeking a new bastion of power to wage the crusade for man's final victory against inhumanity. This is the need of the hour; the priority of the poor. The conference that I envisage will have one and only one iron-clad criterion for inclusion: the non-developed and oppressed community of the Third World. Whether aligned or non-aligned, communist or non-communist, white or yellow or black or brown, the nations of Asia, Africa and Latin America will join in this mission and become the harbinger of one world under one law for all humanity.

Rawalpindi
4 September, 1976

Most newly-independent States of Asia and Africa have been involved in a quest for a formula or principle which would give a stable direction to their foreign policies. This has caused acute mental conflict. The two polarities are represented by the imprecisely defined 'non-alignment', on the one side, and by the policy of multilateral alliances with the super powers, on the other. Is this a neat choice which can be easily exercised in the complexity of current international relationships?

Prime Minister Bhutto has been occupied with the problem throughout his political career. This article, which he published in October 1976, recapitulates his and Pakistan's experience of dealing with powers, great and small, and expresses his considered view of the issue.

BILATERALISM

As a concept, the guiding principle of Pakistan's foreign policy which we call Bilateralism suffers from no confusion or complexity. The idea of conducting and developing our relations with each of the great powers on a bilateral basis, identifying areas of cooperation with one without repudiating an alliance with another and thus evolving an internally consistent and integrated policy requires no justification and implies no moral pretense. The normal mode of maintaining relations between any two countries, great or small, is to base them on their joint perception of their mutual interest. Abstracted from the realities and pressures of our turbulent age, Bilateralism is not a new-fangled notion. The experience, however, of injecting this principle into the body of a country's external relations reveals a certain organic growth. It unfolds important implications and corollaries of the idea which are not always clearly perceived. Having been associated with this experience in government from 1958, I feel that these implications are of more than ephemeral interest. When an idea is sloganized, its original rationale or its concomitants tend to become nebulous. Its edges are blurred, its nuances

31

eclipsed. To put the concept of Bilateralism in perspective, therefore, it is necessary that we recall the changes in the global environment of Pakistan's nascency, early development and maturity and review the adjustments that Pakistan and other Third World countries made to them.

2

This review has to be preceded by the statement of an obvious fact. Even a silhouette of Bilateralism will remain indistinct if it is thought to cover the entire spectrum of a country's external relations. The formation of collective loyalties by sovereign states and their willing acceptance, in whatever degree, of consequent obligations is one of the characteristics of the contemporary world order. A state's membership of the United Nations and its declared adherence to the United Nations Charter, which is now a mark of national independence, engages it constructively in a multilateral relationship. Likewise, on a lower juridical plane and with a relatively limited scope, there exist other associations of states which are formed without any duress or *diktat*. These are generally based on historical background, spiritual or cultural affiliation, geographical contiguity or community of economic interest. For Pakistan, its membership of the Islamic Conference, its bonds with Iran and Turkey and its links with Saudi Arabia as the cradle of Islam govern a considerable segment of its external relations. Then, there are the causes of the emancipation of states from alien subjugation, the ending of usurpation or dominance and hegemony to which Pakistan cannot ideologically forswear its allegiance. The cause of the Arab world, Africa's struggle against racism or residual colonialism and the general interest of the Third World in the establishment of an equitable economic order cannot but decisively influence our attitudes towards international issues and, to that extent, mould our external relationships.

Honouring these obligations is axiomatic and outside the

scope of Bilateralism. Indeed, insofar as all these orientations derive from objectively commendable principles, there is nothing in the concept of Bilateralism which postulates a change in them. Bilateralism would degenerate into sheer opportunism if it meant a deviation from principles, not to speak of their renunciation. What I envision as a correct stance for states with a quantum of power similar to ours is a dignified posture. Not a vestige of dignity can be retained if a state were to lose its foothold on principle and let itself be buffeted by changing expediencies. I have enjoined as an element of policy on the practitioners of our diplomacy that a developing nation's bulwark against the pressures of the great powers is its unwavering adherence to principles and its capacity to articulate them in a given contingency. The notion is demonstrably false that a great power, *qua* a great power, remains beyond conversion to a principle which it might not itself have espoused. In the contemporary age, when international issues arise that bear upon human destiny, the policy untenable for a nation is one of alienation from principles.

3

Political commentators have written volumes on the unique historical situation that crystallized after the Second World War and, for us, coincided with our attainment of independence. The fundamental differences between the new world order and all its predecessors in history were the emergence of two global powers – the United States and the Soviet Union – and their respective identification with two opposite ideologies, each asserting its universal scope, each attempting to propagate itself not only doctrinally but institutionally in other states and each thus seeking to construct a world system of its own choice.

Humanity, of course, had known ecumenical empires before. In the age of empires, however, a great power's dominance was regional and, even with religious sanction, could not cross the limits of the interests of another great power. This was true even of that most expansive of empires, the British Empire, which had to contend with the imperial ambitions of France, Spain and Portugal and, subsequently, of Tsarist Russia, Germany and Japan. As a consequence, at certain crucial stages in its career, the British Empire imposed geographical limits on itself, not out of any constraints on its physical capacity to expand but through acquiescence in the manoeuvres of other imperialist powers.

But, in the era after the Second World War, the two super powers tried to girdle the earth and, in so doing, confronted each other virtually in every part of the globe, on the plane of ideology, commerce, diplomacy or wars by proxy. Each of the two protagonists commanded assets unpossessed by previous great powers; each inhabited territory of a near-continental size; each disposed of unprecedented material resources; each aimed at technological excellence and each professed an assertive ideology. Since neither power ostensibly approved of orthodox imperialism – that is, jurisdiction over other nations' territories through either direct and permanent military occupation or the forced submission of their rulers – their conflict was conducted on a different plane. Their aim was not to subjugate the world in the conventional sense but to control the destinies of nations through a multitude of powerful devices, some open, others invisible, aided by the operation of class interests in other societies and the pervasive influence of the mass media of communication. The contest for global supremacy that took the shape of the Cold War was something to which history offered no parallel.

4

If the bi-polarity which was the most striking feature of this situation had been unqualified, the choice before most developing nations and even quasi-great powers in their external relations would have been narrowed to stark either-or terms. Their options would have been reduced to two; side with one super power or the other; be a satellite or an adversary; genuflect or defy; surrender or offer battle. They would have had little latitude for their contacts and less chance of retaining their independence in its plenitude.

In the mysterious ways of Providence, of which history is but a demonstration, the very process which led to the emergence of the two global powers also generated forces that reduced and even precluded these powers' mastery of the globe. Three developments occurred, not causally related one to another, which had the convergent effect of ridding humanity of the asphyxiation that it might have suffered otherwise. In rough chronological order, these were the formation of the United Nations, the emancipation of China and the liquidation of Western colonialism. But for these, the semi-theological categories of the Cold War would have imposed a dreadful simplification on the world, and human diversity in the working of international affairs would have been denied.

It was, however, many years before all the ramifications of these three phenomena were clearly seen. As the Cold War persisted in its venom and vehemence, the urgent question before the states which were neither incorporated in the Leninist-socialist system nor belonged to the Western Christian civilization was how to conduct their affairs in such a manner as to protect their independence, sovereignty and territorial integrity. In more concrete terms, how would they regain their options? How would they preserve some freedom in shaping their relations with the super powers as well as with others? They could take little comfort in the normative principle, enshrined in the Charter of the United Nations, of the sovereign equality of states. The relationship between a global power and a smaller state could not, in actual fact, be a relationship between equals; the one could extract multiple advantages from the other without responding in sufficient measure,

35

especially when it was engaged in a global contest. Was there no other relationship possible between a super power and a smaller state than that of principal and client?

The bulk of the nations of Asia and Africa, especially the newly-independent states, made an instinctive and honourable response to this situation by choosing the path called non-alignment. For the vast majority of them, it was the only possible way in which they could assert their nationalism, preserve their identity, maintain a flexibility of action in their relationship with all powers, great or small, escape an identification with the total strategic interests of one super power at the expense of the other's interests and thus collectively restore some equilibrium to an otherwise unbalanced world.

On the whole, non-alignment has been a balancing force. As practised by the majority of Asian-African states it has gained the recognition, which it had merited from the beginning, of being morally the only valid and practically the only effective policy available to them in the face of the rivalry of the great powers. But there has been a canker in the rose. This has been generated by the assumed or professed leadership of the group of non-aligned states by one or more powers that have sought to use non-alignment as a lever for their own diplomacy in pursuance of their own chauvinistic ends. When championed by such powers, non-alignment suffers a distortion and does not reflect the strength which the very number and sincerity of most of its adherents would have imparted to it. Divested of its original meaning and purpose, it can become an instrument of national aggrandisement, a subtle weapon for the promotion of a political hegemony by certain powers and the elimination of rivals within their sphere. In such a case, non-alignment would be vulnerable to the criticism that it carries a patent contradiction within itself. The moment non-aligned countries concert their policies under the leadership of one or more countries aspiring to a great power or quasi-great power status, an alignment crystallizes and they cease to be

non-aligned in the sense of not aggravating confusion or disequilibrium in international relations. Happily, this realization
has begun to influence the non-aligned movement.

Jawaharlal Nehru made an historic contribution to the evolution of world affairs by articulating the principle of non-
alignment. By virtue of India's size, importance and intellect,
this contribution would have been an enduring service to
peace if he had not also sought to graft on the movement the
tendency to hammer away at other Third World countries
that had chosen, for compelling reasons, to be aligned with
one or the other of the great powers. This tendency stemmed
from the lamentable fact that India engaged itself in a major
international dispute with its neighbour, Pakistan, in which it
actively sought, and depended upon, the support of a super
power in defying the resolutions of the United Nations. To
seek the help of a super power in promoting the purposes, or
enforcing the decisions, of the United Nations does not vitiate
non-alignment; to seek it for frustrating them most certainly
does. I mention only in passing here the two facts that India
initiated an armed conflict with China and, some years later,
entered into a treaty of a military character with the Soviet
Union. Little wonder that, in such hands, the concept of non-
alignment is translated from the amorphous to the incompre-
hensible.

A state's tendency to browbeat and morally bully its rival is
corrosive to international relationships. In the case of non-
alignment the tendency, whether evinced by India's attempts
to ostracize Pakistan or by the hostility of Nasserist Egypt to
certain other Arab regimes which was visible at the Bandung
Conference in 1955, warps the content of the idea and prevents
this body of Asian-African-Latin American states from providing a new focal point of their collective strength. A closely
related factor which diminished the cohesion of the non-aligned
movement during a historical phase was the tendency, again on
the part not of the non-aligned states as such but of one country,

to play off one super power against the other in the hope of elevating itself to the position of being the indispensable broker between the two and thus playing a great-power role. This was based on the assumption that, without its intercession, there could not be a dialogue or detente between the super powers. It is significant that as early as 1963, in his speech to the United Nations General Assembly, President Tito referred to the changed international situation and said that, in view of it, 'the term non-alignment' had 'been rendered somewhat obsolete by new positive trends in international relations'.

I believe that the still valid concept of non-alignment can be saved from both obsolescence and negativity if the group of non-aligned states remains consistent in forswearing the promotion of expansionist national objectives and also provides a fair and logical answer to certain questions about its composition. By doing so, it will recapture its original terms of reference which forbid an interventionist role that would divide the countries of the Third World and dissipate their total limited strength.

First, what is the principle of inclusion in the ranks of the non-aligned? Does non-alignment mean that there can be bilateral military alignments with Eastern states but there cannot be any alliances of Asian or African countries with the West? The criterion which is based on the distinction between multilateral alliances and bilateral treaties is illusive because both such engagements are either equally innocuous or equally part of the pattern of great-power rivalries. Then again, it is apparent that, despite a diversity in ideological moorings, political systems and economic conditions, the non-aligned movement derives its force from the experience of colonial domination common to all its members. How can, therefore, those states be excluded which have suffered from the same experience and are equally engaged in the struggle to end the iniquities in the international economy? Secondly, the original terms of reference of the non-aligned movement implied an equi-distant position from both the super powers and a scrupulous avoidance of using non-alignment as a pressure grouping against neighbours. But when a country enters into closer relations with one great power and still professes to be non-aligned in order to be better able to establish its political domination over a neighbouring country then what we witness is alignment masquerading as non-alignment. Such an arrangement is *ultra vires* of the concept of non-alignment.

These questions relate organically to both the concept and the practical expression of non-alignment. If non-alignment is to become a movement of great value once again, it has to restore its pristine image, redefine its objectives and redetermine its priorities. International affairs have now reached a stage when non-alignment cannot afford to limit its votaries to certain high priests and those they regard as their disciples. If other Third World countries are kept beyond the pale, the transcendental issue of world affairs today would be eclipsed. This is the issue of the division between the exploiters and the exploited, regardless of geographical location, power alignment, race, religion or ideology. In itself not a political contrivance, the division cannot be manipulated for the promotion of any country's specific national policy. The issue demands a mobilization of the energies of the Third World, hitherto unfocussed, not for a conflict with the richer countries but for the dismantling of iniquities, not for the destruction of a particular system but for the building of a new economic order through rectification of existing imbalances. Any movement, any grouping, any manoeuvre that retards the unification of the Third World for achieving this pre-eminently just end will invoke the censure of being little-minded, of ignoring the historical situation and of blocking a radical but constructive response to the challenge of the times.

It is with this consideration that I have recently issued an appeal for convening a conference of the developing countries of Asia, Africa and Latin America at the summit level. I am convinced that the idea of an inclusive forum of the Third World will be perceived as an enlargement and evolution, and not as a negation, of the concept of non-alignment.

5

I have not felt the need to be apologetic about the agreements or understandings of mutual defence and cooperation that have existed between Pakistan and the United States. Insofar as they are intrinsically consistent with Pakistan's self-interest, untainted with any dishonourable motive, directed against no other power's legitimate interests and as they do not fetter Pakistan's standpoints nor hamper its loyalty to the causes of Asia and Africa, Pakistan is under no necessity of repudiating these agreements merely to establish its credentials as a member of the Third World and a promoter of its supreme aims. These credentials are the vital tissue of the organism of a state that was born in a glorious struggle which carried the force of a thousand years of history, of a nation inhabiting the heart of Asia, of a people authentically Asian in their personality, of a country situated in the immediate proximity of China and the Soviet Union and of a society sharing the culture and civilization of the Middle East.

What for a certain time obscured these realities was not any agreement with the West but the way it was interpreted by one side or understood by the other. The result was that, for a time, Pakistan found itself maladjusted to its world environment and the Asian-African situation. The impression was created that Pakistan wished to escape its geography, falsify its identity, ignore its long-term interests and barter away the freedom of choice without which independence is but a myth. If I have sought to do anything in our external affairs, it has been not only to dispel this impression but also to lend an authenticity to our foreign policy. A foreign policy is inauthentic if it does not articulate a nation's psychic urges or reflect an awareness of the historical process. The struggle to add this dimension of depth to the totality of our external relationships has not been an easy one.

Intrinsically, there is nothing repugnant to the values and objectives of the common cause of the Third World if an Asian, African or Latin American country enters into an alliance with either the East or the West. An element of repugnance is introduced by discrimination and non-reciprocity.

I shall not analyse here the causes of Pakistan's entanglement during the 1950s in situations which were as anomalous as they were inimical to its national interest. To be fair to all those who managed the nation's affairs at that time, the motive force was a quest for security. Alone among the newly-independent major states, Pakistan was born embattled. As early as two months after its establishment, the Founder of Pakistan, Quaid-i-Azam Mohammad Ali Jinnah, who was not given to exaggeration, felt constrained to talk of 'a well-organized and well-directed' plot to force Pakistan 'to come into the (Indian) Union as a penitent, repentant, erring son' and, to that end, 'to paralyze the new-born state'. This he said on 24 October 1947, three days before India sent her troops to Kashmir, to prevent that state's rightful accession to Pakistan. It is, therefore, hardly surprising that Pakistan's overriding concern in the early years was the security of the country. This was at a time when the United States was nonpareil and promised not only a firmer military underpinning than could be obtained from any other quarter but large and generous economic assistance. With the added, and enduring, factor of a facility of dialogue with the United States, the consequent alliance could not be deemed unnatural.

While these factors cannot be ignored, it would be falsification of history to dismiss on this account the contradictions in which Pakistan continually involved itself in conducting its external affairs. Some examples are most pertinent.

Pakistan was among the states which recognized the People's

Republic of China soon after its establishment. Yet, some years later, while still maintaining the recognition, it persistently voted in the United Nations against the immediate representation of China by its legitimate and recognized government.* In 1956, despite the first journey of a Prime Minister of Pakistan to China and on the eve of Prime Minister Chou En-lai's return visit, Pakistan still supported action to exclude the representatives of the People's Republic of China from the United Nations. When in September-October 1958 a clash over Taiwan seemed possible, Pakistan went so far as to disregard the implications of its own recognition of the People's Republic of China and conveyed the message to the Chinese that 'the juridical position of sovereignty over Formosa' was not clear.†

On 2 June 1949, the USSR conveyed an invitation to the Prime Minister of Pakistan to visit Moscow. The invitation was accepted and announced but, when the Soviet Union suggested the exchange of Ambassadors between the two countries prior to the Prime Minister's visit, it was officially stated in Pakistan that the exchange could not be achieved immediately due to 'a shortage of personnel' in Karachi.‡ While Moscow's invitation was thus virtually spurned, a later invitation from Washington, which had the appearance of an after-thought, was promptly accepted. In April 1950, the visit to the Soviet Union was shelved, only to materialize fifteen years later after many changes of government in Pakistan and a considerable transformation of the international scene.

These contradictions surfaced not only in Pakistan's relations with the great powers. What was its attitude towards the Islamic world? On the one side, the national leadership at the time made the claim that Pakistan was 'the fortress of Islam'. On the other, a former Prime Minister, referring to the Muslim

* See Notes, pp. 105–6.
† See Notes, p. 106.
‡ See Notes, p. 107.

42

countries, delivered the celebrated verdict that 'zero plus zero plus zero still equals zero'.* On the one side, with Pakistan's leadership of the campaign against the dismemberment of Palestine in 1947, there were protestations of undying support to the Arab cause. On the other, Pakistan adopted a policy of dither and equivocation over the historic Suez Canal issue in 1956.

These are but a few outstanding examples of the kind of thinking which governed Pakistan's foreign policy and which I had encountered in the first meeting on the subject held under Ayub Khan's presidentship.† None could be ascribed to an objective concern with security. Other elements played their part. There was the fact of Pakistan's inexperience in international affairs. Who but a novitiate would expect that, by providing the Bada Ber surveillance base to the United States, India would be made to 'disgorge' Kashmir? It was this base which figured in the famous U-2 incident in 1960 and provoked the public threat from Nikita Khruschev that the Soviet forces would wipe out Peshawar.‡ A US Senator visited this base, asked a Pakistani official what compensation Pakistan had received for it and, on hearing the reply, remarked, 'You Pakistanis are suckers. For less important bases, hundreds of millions are given.' In addition to the element of naïveté, there was a lack of integrity in a national leadership which was tied to the interests of a limited class of entrepreneurs and bureaucrats and, therefore, removed from the people's urges and aspirations. The offer of Pakistani troops to fight in Laos in 1961, reminiscent of an earlier half-suppressed thought relating to Korea in 1951, was a proof that the country's rulers regarded its soldiers as no more than cannon-fodder. Such a ruling class, itself incapable of understanding the historical situation, is prone to psychological projection and apt to imagine that the

* See Notes, pp. 107–8.
† See Notes, pp. 108–9.
‡ See Notes, pp. 109–10.

43

other side is equally unsophisticated. Only this explains Ayub Khan's resounding promise, in his address to the US Congress in 1961, that Pakistan would one day be the only country in Asia to stand by America.* Not realizing what this implied, Pakistan's ruling class was wont to express surprise that, in the Asian-African environment, the country had been relegated to a political quarantine.

6

The crowning absurdity of this state of affairs was revealed in October-November 1959. At that time, reports were already available of a dispute between China and India about an area in Ladakh, in the territory of the Jammu and Kashmir State. On 23 October 1959, however, President Ayub Khan addressed a press conference at which he dwelt on 'the serious threat from the north', said that 'events on the Tibet border would make the subcontinent militarily vulnerable' and emphasized the necessity of India and Pakistan coming together to meet the danger.† He followed this by a statement made in an airport interview on 3 November about 'the latest Chinese incursion in Ladakh', saying that it was 'India's problem'‡. On 8 November, he was again reported to have said that 'Chinese occupation of Tibet' was posing 'a serious threat from the north'. It must be remembered in this context that China had notably resisted all Indian blandishments in the heyday of Sino-Indian friendship and refused to support India's claim to Jammu and Kashmir.

I was not in charge of the country's foreign affairs at the time. In New York, leading the Pakistan delegation to the General Assembly, I was filled with a sense of foreboding at these reports. It was not only that the head of Pakistan's government was making an offer of joint defence to India which only those

* See Notes, p. 110.
† See Notes, pp. 110–12.
‡ See Notes, p. 112.

unlettered in international affairs would hope to be accepted or reciprocated. That was humiliating enough. What was dangerous was that, in the process, he was serving notice to China of Pakistan's hostility and, in addition, lending sanction to India's claim to Kashmir, the very claim which Pakistan had challenged through all the years and the United Nations had refused to recognize. This was how Pakistan's interpretation of the alliance with the United States was damaging its enduring national interests.

Realizing how hard it would be to unlock the government from this self-stultifying, indeed suicidal, position, how a frontal attack on the then prevailing philosophy would be parried and how much tact would be necessary to wean the country away from the stance it had adopted, I addressed a letter to Ayub Khan immediately after reading these press reports. In this letter dated 11 November 1959, I reminded him that, by 'the statements we have made' and 'the entire attitude' we had evinced, we could be taken to have tacitly recognized India's authority over the part of Kashmir under its occupation and to justify any augmentation of Indian forces in Kashmir, contrary to the United Nations resolutions. I then suggested an authoritative pronouncement, possibly in the form of a letter to the Security Council, safeguarding Pakistan against these dangers. China may not, I added, 'react adversely to a statement from Pakistan questioning the very basis of the stand taken by India regarding Ladakh'. I also sent a copy of this letter to Foreign Minister Manzur Qadir and suggested to him that we 'examine the whole question in depth and not let the India-China situation regarding Kashmir drift and develop to our detriment'.*

President Ayub Khan realized how he would be denounced by the people if he appeared to have weakened Pakistan's position on Jammu and Kashmir. Changing his tune upon the receipt of my letter, he stated on 23 November that Pakistan would not recognize any arrangement between India and

* See Notes, pp. 112–15.

45

China in Ladakh as the area was a disputed territory between
Pakistan and India.* As suggested by me, he also authorized
our Permanent Representative at the United Nations to address
a letter to the President of the Security Council which reserved
Pakistan's position and declared that 'pending a determination
of the future of Kashmir through the will of the people impartially ascertained, no positions taken or adjustments made by
either of the parties to the present controversy between India
and China, or any similar controversy in the future, shall affect
the status of the territory of Jammu and Kashmir or the
imperatives of the demilitarization and self-determination of
the State'. The letter added that it would be 'for the sovereign
authority freely evolved by the people of Jammu and Kashmir
to effect, or refuse to effect, any adjustment of its frontiers with
any foreign power'.†

While seemingly centred on the restricted question of
Jammu and Kashmir, this was the first demonstration by
Pakistan of its capacity to maintain its national position in a
contingency even when such maintenance ran counter to the
tactical considerations weighing with the great power with
which it had allied itself. As I envisioned it, such a course of
action would not connote any weakening, far less a termination,
of the alliance. All that it would indicate was that the smaller
party in the alliance would not suffer its national interests to
be overlaid. In this way, the alliance would gain strength by
an infusion of realism and equity. An alliance is but a tissue of
strains and frictions, of no benefit to either side, if it submerges
the interests of the smaller partner. It acquires solidity when
it reassures the one that needs such reassurance that his
interests will be duly protected and advanced.

A year later, on 14 October 1960, I wrote to Foreign Minister
Manzur Qadir about Pakistan's vote on the question of Chinese

---

* See Notes, pp. 115–16.
† See Notes, pp. 116–17.

representation at the United Nations.* This vote was becoming preposterous and earning no respect for Pakistan from nations not wedded to the Cold War. I wrote that I could not see why Pakistan should not be considered a staunch ally, any less than certain countries (Norway and Denmark) which had voted against the US, if it took 'a stand on the merits of the question and a recognition of realities'. This led to a Cabinet discussion in November 1960 at which it was decided to support China's legitimate representation at the United Nations.† It is a matter of history how these small beginnings led to bigger results in the form of establishing contacts with China, negotiating and concluding a boundary agreement with her and opening the era of cordiality and close friendship between Pakistan and her great neighbour.

Along with establishing contacts with China, I was also feeling the necessity of initiating a dialogue with the Soviet Union. Immediately after my return from the United Nations in October 1960, as Minister for Fuel, Power and Natural Resources, I announced my intention to go to Moscow to discuss the possibility of Soviet assistance to Pakistan in the exploitation of our oil and mineral resources.‡ The terrain was roughened for me by my own government. Some influential members of Ayub Khan's cabinet counselled that the visit would be 'inadvisable'. When persistent arguments broke the resistance, the key man in my delegation, who had gone to Delhi, claimed to be sick. Another of my principal advisers was instructed not to stay with me in Moscow for more than a few days. I was directed to return home a day before the agreement which had been evolved was to be signed. It was finally signed by me and the Soviet Ambassador in Karachi. But for this purblind attitude of Pakistan's erstwhile rulers towards the Soviet Union, on the one side, and the regrettable trend in Soviet

* See Notes, pp. 117–19.
† See Notes, pp. 120–21.
‡ See Notes, pp. 121–22.

policy of closely associating Soviet interests with India's in our region, on the other, the beginning I had attempted in 1960 could have paved the way for an uninterrupted course of friendly and fruitful relations between the two countries.

7

I need hardly narrate here the whole story of international developments directly involving Pakistan between 1960 and 1966. For a time, especially in 1963–64 and up to the war of September 1965, Pakistan sought to regain its capacity to respond to the dynamics of the world situation and remove itself from a narrow, one-dimensional, all-or-nothing basis of relationship with great powers. On a visit to the subcontinent in 1962, Dr Kissinger had observed that America had been suffering from 'pactitis'. The observation, based on a keen perception of an evolving world situation, could no longer be ignored. A national personality programmed to react to signals from one source alone could be an asset neither to itself nor to its allies. For its own benefit and in the larger interest of restoring a balance to our region, Pakistan decided to activate its diplomatic arteries with both China and the Soviet Union. These channels had remained open although few cordial communications had earlier flowed through them. During the India–China conflict in 1962, there were representatives of certain vested interests in Pakistan who wanted to allow American military equipment to be moved to India through Pakistan. The time had arrived to thwart the designs of such interests.

This progress was, however, arrested by two sets of developments. One was the considerable pressure put on Pakistan by the obsessive hostility of the Lyndon Johnson administration in the US towards China and by the pressures it exerted to force a change in Pakistan's policy. Such was the extent of the suspicion with which that administration viewed every move regarding China that, in August 1963, it suspended a $4.3 million loan for the Dacca airport because Pakistan had signed a civil aviation agreement with China. The cancellation in April 1965 of an invitation to Ayub Khan to visit the United States, the postponement in July 1965 of the Aid-to-Pakistan Consortium meeting, the imposition of an arms embargo during the India–Pakistan war of 1965 which operated to the direct detriment of Pakistan and not of India, the warning to China on 16 September 1965 against helping Pakistan – all these were actions against the policy of dialogue and friendship with China.

The other set of developments, paralleling the first but traceable to a similar source, was the Soviet attitude in the Pakistan–India War of September 1965 and the insurance of the Tashkent Declaration in January 1966.

Neither of these chains of events would have confused Pakistan's foreign policy if the country had a leadership which understood the complexity of international relations and could maintain a serenity and a steadiness despite temporary setbacks. It is ironical that the correctness of Pakistan's policy towards China was vindicated for the United States by subsequent developments in the world situation – but, thanks to the ineptitude of a junta in Pakistan, at Pakistan's colossal expense. As far back as 1965–66, I had conveyed to President Johnson and Secretary of State Rusk that Pakistan could serve as a bridge between China and the United States. When, in a conversation I had with Dean Rusk in Ankara, this possibility was explored, Ayub Khan took alarm and said that we should not 'burn our fingers'.* More than fingers were burnt when, in 1971 – five crucial, destructive years after I had first put forth the proposition – Yahya Khan's regime made arrangements for Dr Kissinger to fly through Pakistan on his secret mission to Peking. The event itself, the inception of a direct dialogue between China and the United States, could not have

* See Notes, pp. 122–24.

been more felicitous for Pakistan. 'Do not forget the bridge which you crossed in coming here,' Premier Chou En-lai said to Dr Kissinger in Peking. But, from Pakistan's side, the development fell into a context – the civil war in East Pakistan and tensions on the border with India – which provoked the kind of speculation that could easily have been avoided if parallel approaches had been made to reassure the Soviet Union. In the actual setting, the immediate sequel to Dr Kissinger's journey through Rawalpindi to Peking was the *coup de grace* dealt by the signing of the Indo-Soviet Treaty in August 1971, the draft of which had remained under consideration for three years. Nothing but this treaty enabled India to launch its armed invasion of East Pakistan in November 1971.

The relationship between Pakistan and China has withstood the stress of that and other lesser developments. Its strength lies in its sincerity on both sides. But the essence of Bilateralism is that a sincere relationship need not be converted into an *affaire de coeur* which disregards circumspection and imposes a strain on both sides.

Some years earlier, after the Tashkent Declaration in 1966, Ayub Khan made some rather disingenuous attempts to laud the Soviet Union for its intervention. This showed that, though he was persuaded of the necessity of establishing friendly relations with China and the Soviet Union, he did not grasp the basic principle that Bilateralism flows from the sum of relations between two countries and does not hinge on a single development. My standpoint, which I stated in official memoranda, was that good relations with the great powers should not be made dependent on each and every initiative either in favour or otherwise, for then there would be no continuity or certainty in state relations.* But in a setting where the approach to international issues is temperamental, pleadings of this kind remain unheeded. I may mention here the personal fact that,

* See Notes, pp. 124–30.

witnessing a drift in Pakistan's policy and finding fruitless my
expositions of Bilateralism, I resigned as Foreign Minister in
1966.

8

During the years that have elapsed since, there have occurred
some global developments which, in a historical perspective, are
almost of the same magnitude as the three (the establishment
of the United Nations, the liquidation of colonialism and
the emergence of China) which I mentioned earlier. Briefly,
these are: first, the reassertion of nationalism not only in the
Third World but also in the Western and Socialist worlds;
second, the achievement, despite current difficulties, of
economic prosperity in Europe, Japan, the Socialist world and
the oil-producing countries, which has led to a dispersion of
centres of power and, third, the policy of detente between the
United States and the Soviet Union following the attainment of
nuclear parity by them. All these have created an objective
world situation in which the terrain for the exercise of Bilateralism is not only smoother but which has made Bilateralism essentially the ground on which a developing nation can base its
contacts with great powers. For Pakistan, there has been the
phenomenon of its resurgence after the shattering events of
1971. Were it not for this revival, I would not be expounding
the constituent principles of what I regard as a viable foreign
policy.

A pre-requisite of clean and consistent bilateral relations is
the substance of non-alignment in the sense that the relations
are confined to the limits of the common national interests of
the two powers concerned and do not exceed these limits
inimically to the interest of a third country. This provokes the
question how bilateral relations can be maintained by a smaller
state with a global power when the latter's tactical or strategic
interests are opposed to the former's national interest in a

certain situation. The answer is that this point of conflict can be insulated in direct dealings with the great power concerned and a workable equilibrium sought independent of this point, provided, of course, the segregation of the conflicting interest is scrupulously mutual and reciprocal. By removing, as far as it can, the point of conflict from the channel of a direct and barren encounter, the smaller state retains the freedom to vindicate its stand. This it can do by mobilizing the moral support of world opinion which can persuade the great power concerned to alter its position in its own independent interest.*

This implies a gradation of relationships but with the minimum of strain or tension. The gradation is determined by the degree of recognition a state receives of its position of principles on major international problems in which it is directly involved. If a state were to ignore the help and support which it has received from one power and try to maintain as much cordiality or correctness with it as with another power that has withheld such assistance, then it would cease to command respect and would forfeit its credit. When a state does not impose support on contentious issues as a pre-condition on the exploration of other avenues of mutual cooperation, it does not thereby declare that such support has no relevance to the level, degree of warmth or intimacy of state relations.

Reciprocity is thus the obverse of the coin. When a smaller state seeks its relations with the great powers to be consistent, when it does not let relations with one cut across the ambit and scope of relations with another, when it refrains from predetermined partiality in a great-power conflict, it expects a basic reciprocity from the other side. A commitment of policy in state relations cannot be one-sided. It is not equitable that a smaller state should impose a self-denying ordinance on itself without a similar response from the other side in the bilateral relationship. Such relationships must reflect agreement on certain fundamental principles between the two states. Other-

* See Notes, pp. 124–30.

wise, the smaller state can be reduced to a pitiable satellite and Bilateralism will degenerate into a baneful alignment.

The irreducible minimum of reciprocity is mutual respect for each other's territorial integrity and sovereignty and non-interference in each other's internal affairs. This hardly needs to be elaborated. There are few countries in the world that have not subscribed to these principles which are enshrined in the Charter of the United Nations, the Declaration on World Peace and Cooperation issued by the Bandung Conference in 1955 and numerous other texts of international law. It is difficult to see how two states can have any kind of relations unless they are prepared to accept the geographical boundaries of each other's national territory, acknowledge each other's sovereignty and undertake not to interfere in each other's internal affairs. But, in the very nature of things, this obligation rests more heavily on the great power than on the smaller one in a bilateral relationship, for it is not the smaller power which can question the great power's state frontiers or try to interfere in its internal affairs. The great power itself may not do so but it may acquiesce in, or encourage, situations in which doubt is cast on the smaller power's territorial integrity or its right to deter-mine its own affairs. It is one thing for the smaller state to segregate from mutual relations those questions on which the perceptions of the two countries differ and to try to prevent the difference from spilling over into the broader areas where agreement exists. It is altogether another to suffer a compro-mise, or turn the other cheek, when matters as fundamental as territorial integrity or political independence are involved. No one can take pride in bilateral relations with adversaries whose policies run counter to his basic interests. Moreover, there cannot be an equivalence in what is called *quid pro quo* in bilateral relations between states of unequal international stature. To the degree that the one commands wider inter-national influence and disposes of a larger quantum of power, its return for the other's friendly cooperation has to be greater.

Every act which denotes a withholding of this return will call for a corresponding and measured response. The relationship may not be severed but the necessary conclusion will be drawn and a different pattern will be evolved.

9

An intermediate question arises here: can an alliance between a great power and a developing nation remain intact in a bilateralist scheme of foreign policy? The answer is in the affirmative but the question could be nagging only if one were to ignore the entire thrust of decades of effort by the great powers backed by the counsel and importunities of world opinion. Since the whole objective of this effort has been to establish a *modus vivendi* between the super powers and since also the contingency of a war between them, which would mean total annihilation, recedes farther from reality, the first duty of a party to a defence alliance with a great power relating to the eventuality of an all-out war involving that great power does not have the imminence and the urgency to pervade all diplomatic approaches and understandings towards cooperation and peace. This is so regardless of a country adopting a bilateralist stance or otherwise.

There have also been other developments in the international situation which govern the interpretation of alliances equally on both sides. The invention of inter-continental ballistic missiles a decade and a half ago brought about changes in military strategy as a result of which the original concept of peripheral defence was modified and the importance of military pacts, insofar as they were based on that concept, was altered. In a changed environment, the original scenario of pacts creating power amalgams or consolidating various nations into units of total power inevitably underwent a drastic revision. Again, Bilateralism was not the agent but the product of this change.

Moreover, the proposition that Bilateralism is not incompatible with alliances is backed by the visible phenomenon that alliances do not constitute all-embracing, categorical imperatives for either side. They do not chart a straight and narrow path of compliance from which the smaller state is not permitted to deviate; if they did, diplomacy would be denuded of its moral content and purpose. Thus, there is a large room for the exercise of their own diplomacy by states in accordance with what they perceive as their national interest. In order to endure and to escape anomalies and irritations, an alliance has to accommodate the interests of both sides. Here again, however, the accommodation cannot be equal. The vital interests of a great power are secured by its very greatness while those of a smaller state associated with an alliance may be in jeopardy without that alliance. Were the associated state to acquiesce in the shelving of its deep concerns and accept a position of *diktat*, what insurance could it have that, in the dynamics of international affairs, the dominant state would not at some stage consider the alliance obsolete?

This leads to a two-fold conclusion: first, Bilateralism does not *per se* repudiate alliances with the great powers; second, the combination of a bilateralist stance and an adherence to an alliance does create difficulties in the actual conduct of international affairs. The difficulties and the strain are accentuated in situations where a particular alliance system or organization, divorced from the bilateral agreements or understandings between its members, has lost the cohesion and strength envisaged for it in a different historical situation. What Bilateralism seeks to do is, firstly, to fasten on those elements in an alliance which remain relevant through all the changes in the global environment and, depending on reciprocity, carry out the obligations flowing from them and, secondly, to demarcate the area which is not covered by these elements and exercise the state's options in it. What determines this exercise?

It goes without saying that a country is primarily actuated by its national interest. But where the impingement of an international issue on this interest may be uncertain or doubtful and where the interest itself may be open to question, the only yardstick for judging an issue is its merits. I know that every party to a dispute holds that the merits of the case are on its side. But I assert that this is no reason why merits should be cynically disregarded. There are objective criteria for determining them. These are furnished by (i) the established principles of international law; (ii) the resolutions of the United Nations; (iii) treaty obligations; (iv) the accordance or variance of a party's standpoint on the dispute with both its own previous statements or declarations and the settled position of other governments on similar issues in other contexts; (v) the readiness or unwillingness of a party to a dispute to have recourse to the methods of peaceful settlement outlined in the Charter of the United Nations and (vi) the recommendations of a regional machinery for the settlement of a dispute which may be established when other criteria do not yield a definite judgement.

There is no need for me to elaborate these criteria as they are exhaustively discussed in the jurisprudence of the United Nations. Much though the world organization presents a spectacle of futility, acute though is the world's loss of faith in its efficacy, the powerlessness of the United Nations is not an argument of an international issue to be judged other than on its merits. If it is not the recommendations or decisions of the United Nations that serve to bring an international situation into alignment with the rightness of a cause, then the task is accomplished, at much greater cost, by the movements of peoples and the operation of historical forces. An active United Nations or not, the future in international affairs can be organized only along the lines of merit. Power politics may distort a right or delay the evolution. But even the contemporary age, with the discouraging examples of Kashmir and Palestine, has not conclusively proved that the fabrications of power politics will not prove flimsy in the long run.

Two disparate examples from Pakistan's current concerns may be pertinent here. One is our dispute with India regarding the disposition of the State of Jammu and Kashmir. We have taken, and we will take, no position on this dispute which does not satisfy objective criteria of merit. The second is the far less vexatious and stubborn question of Pakistan acquiring a re-processing plant and heavy water facilities which, I regret, has been wholly misunderstood by certain elements in the United States.

These elements are, I concede, motivated by a concern about the spread of nuclear weapons beyond the circle of the five nuclear powers. Pakistan shares that concern. If anything, it has more cause for apprehension about the proliferation of nuclear weapons than even the most humane opinion elsewhere. We have repeatedly and voluntarily given categorical assurances about the peaceful intent of our nuclear programme. Lest it be thought that these are just verbal pledges, we have accepted iron-clad IAEA safeguards for every one of our nuclear facilities. We have gone even further and accepted the most stringent conditions from France, the supplier of the re-processing plant, which fully conform to the guidelines adopted by the seven nuclear exporting countries. The agreement for the supply of this plant was accompanied by the conclusion of a trilateral safeguards agreement with IAEA approved by its Board of Governors by consensus. Moreover, we have worked out fail-safe expedients with Canada and the Federal Republic of Germany regarding an atomic reactor and a small heavy water plant respectively. There could not possibly be a more convincing earnest of our commitment to use our nuclear facilities for exclusively peaceful purposes.

Thus, Pakistan's going ahead with its peaceful nuclear

programme is a non-event as far as nuclear proliferation is concerned. That this should be turned into an event while the unrestrained nuclear programmes of Israel, South Africa and India are considered non-events is a dismal commentary on the regard for merits shown by those who ostensibly would not like to ignore them. India is reported to have plans to carry out a series of nuclear explosions, having already conducted one on our doorstep. Her nuclear capability was built on the materials and technology she derived from an unsafeguarded reactor and heavy water supplied by Canada and the United States respectively. Can it be claimed that there is not some discrimination involved here? Does it prove that the nuclear monopoly of the great powers is being judiciously used in the interests of peace and equilibrium? Not only Pakistan but a large number of non-nuclear-weapon states would be gladdened by a convincing assurance on this score.

II

If a developing nation scrupulously forswears any interest in the continuance or exacerbation of a conflict between the great powers, it correspondingly devolves on the great powers not to tacitly approve or aggravate regional imbalances. Only thus can bilateral relations between the great and the developing nations be free from strain. Only thus can that framework of principles be strengthened within which a state can pursue its objectives in external affairs without becoming a liability on a great power, without eroding its associations or repudiating its undertakings. Unpretentiously, Bilateralism provides such a framework.

In matters of men and state, it is not possible to achieve a formulation which takes into account all variables and unforeseen contingencies. Some element of simplification is unavoidable in the quest for the bases of dealing with complicated situations. 'By their fruits, ye shall know them.' Prior to the adoption of Bilateralism, Pakistan's foreign policy was, at worst, capricious and, at best, one of pragmatism planted on a half-forgotten ideology. With the adoption of this principle, Pakistan has steered itself through the treacherous shoals and currents that menace the passage of strategically placed states in the complex, contemporary age. Bilateralism has provided a safe chart for this kind of navigation. More importantly, it has helped Pakistan to fulfil, as well as it can, the Islamic injunction of integrity in international dealings. The injunction is immutable.

Rawalpindi
30 October 1976

The Regional Cooperation for Development between Iran, Pakistan and Turkey was established in 1964 and envisaged a community of economic interests of the three countries which are geographically contiguous.

On the eve of their last Summit Conference in April 1976 at Izmir, Pakistan's Prime Minister Bhutto directed his thoughts, as a student of history, to the development of the association of the three countries in accordance with the historical process.

Earlier, in February 1976, at the Conference of their Foreign Ministers in Lahore, Bhutto had expressed his dissatisfaction at the level of the operation of RCD and called for a mobilization and integration of the collective resources of the three countries.

REGIONAL COOPERATION
FOR DEVELOPMENT

The Izmir Conference will provide a valuable opportunity for the leaders of Iran, Turkey and Pakistan to carry forward the exchange of thoughts which has been in progress at different places in the three countries during the last year. With the candour and cordiality natural in such a brotherhood, this exchange is untainted with prejudice. We have been surveying our entire political, strategic and economic environment and reviewing our adjustments to it. While this survey continues, it would betray an incomprehension of international realities to expect any dramatic or spectacular results from the Izmir Conference. Indeed, in the light of recent discussions at the meeting of the three Commerce Ministers in Teheran, the outcome of the Izmir Conference calls for no prophecy.

However, I am not thinking today of tomorrow's conference only. I am not going to Izmir to propound any thesis which, upon my return, I would expect to serve as an avenue for new interplays in diplomacy. I direct my thought in this engagement more as a student of history than in the discharge of my current responsibilities. My thoughts are not confined to the immediate prospects but to the development of the association of the three countries in tune with the historical process. In this time of epoch-making events, when the destinies of nations stand at the crossroads, I cannot conceal my feelings. A compelling urge requires me to share my thoughts with my countrymen.

2

Iran, Pakistan and Turkey constitute a single civilization. Their cultures are permeated by a common faith. Their historical backgrounds interpenetrate. Their languages bear testimony to shared modes of thought and instinctive responses. Their arts and literatures articulate collective experiences which are cast in the same psychic mould. Their societies are governed by the same sense of values. In reality this civilization has far greater inner cohesion than even the one proudly upheld by the West European community.

The cultural affinity of the three nations is strengthened by certain historical, economic and political phenomena. Unlike the nations of West Europe, no two of us have gone to war against each other in the relevant past. There are no recent memories we have to erase. Nor have our developing economies created the rivalries, or generated the antagonisms, prevalent between industrialized societies. Our concerns for security bear a common stamp as we face similar challenges, actual or potential. Lastly, within the life-span of many living today, none of the three countries has been immune from aggression. Turkey was invaded, and in large part occupied, in the aftermath of the First World War and subjected to intolerable pressures in 1974. Iran saw itself brought under foreign control, with its sovereignty denied and its territory split, during and after the Second World War. Pakistan has been dragged into three wars since 1947; the last of them, aided by an international conspiracy, splintered off its eastern part.

All these factors have generated a sense of community on the popular level which is infinitely stronger than the devices hitherto employed to give it a focus and direction. Is it not a moral obligation of the leadership of the three countries to preserve the love and affection felt by their peoples for one another by establishing a living unity which can withstand the vicissitudes of the contemporary age?

How do we stand today in face of fast-changing global and regional patterns?

3

We have entered an era when a new terminology has emerged supplanting the banal clichés and evocative phrases of the decades of the fifties and sixties. With full-scale nuclear war having ceased to be a viable option, the relations between the two super powers have moved from cold war in the fifties to peaceful co-existence in the sixties to detente in the seventies. Detente is a complex phenomenon. As between the two super powers, it is a relationship which conjointly incorporates the three elements of cooperation, competition and conflict, incipient or chronic; each element coming to the surface as appropriate to a given situation. But in the larger field of international affairs, detente cannot be meaningful for the bulk of the world's nations if it only means that competition, in the military field, is controlled and, and in the political, restrained. What is far more important is that it should create an ethos in which crises in different parts of the world are not manipulated or exploited for the advantage of a super power or its client and no pressure is brought on lesser states to fall in line. Since this has not yet happened, what we see today is a turbulent world scene, characterized, in varying measure, by equilibrium and disequilibrium, isolation and interdependence, co-existence and confrontation.

Current jargon describes it as a multi-polar world. In the

macrocosm, the dispersion of the centres of power may have had a salutary impact on the evolving pattern of international relations. Yet the fact remains that this multi-polarity can potentially stir the hegemonic ambitions of even regional powers which are not subject to the restraints that nuclear parity imposes on the two super powers. The result is that there is a tenuous line, a delicate balance, between stability and chaos. The line can be crossed, and the balance upset, by the military adventure of any assertive regional power which feels the temptation, and obtains the impunity, to launch it against its neighbours. It may make war impelled by its own ambition or acting as a proxy.

This is the dominant characteristic of the current era. Turmoil and tensions seethe beneath a thin layer of tranquillity. There is a flux in place of former fixities. In Europe, the Helsinki Conference may have defined and delimited the region about which there is agreement. But, soon after the conclusion of the Final Act of the Conference, varying interpretations began to be placed on it, each side attaching a greater importance to what it considers its own part of the basket. At any rate, the configuration of a stable order elsewhere is left to be determined by the balance of forces emerging from a possible collision or chance encounter or mutual tolerance or deliberate or unintended parallelism of the two super powers.

4

There is no settled view of the potentialities of the European situation itself, where crises may occur at unforeseen points. As against the view that the relation between the Soviet Union and East Europe should be 'organic', anticipations of dissidence there continue to be made. The possibility of the capture or sharing of power by Communist parties in certain NATO countries has been pronounced to be part of an 'irreversible process' and, therefore, 'inevitable' by a prominent American analyst, a former Under Secretary of State. At the same time, the present Secretary of State has said that the development would be unacceptable as it would weaken, if not undermine, the political solidarity and collective defence of the West embodied in NATO. Following such a development, he has added, 'the commitment of the American people to maintain the balance of power in Europe, justified though it might be on pragmatic, geopolitical grounds, would lack the moral base on which it has stood for thirty years'. While denying the inevitability of such an occurrence, the US Secretary of State has said that it would mark 'a historic turning point in Atlantic relations'. The strains on the alliance in the eastern Mediterranean are also not a negligible fact. Thus, not to speak of other regions, Europe, politically the maturest of all, raises questions to which the older equations provide no answer.

The Middle East continues to be the area of the most perilous tension. An appraisal, to be valid, must take into account not only the slackening, because of an inherent weakness, of the peace efforts but also a multiplicity of other phenomena. These would include the level and quality of the Western response to Egypt's situation, the protracted agony of Lebanon, the dispute over the Sahara, the introduction of a nuclear threat by Israel and the unfortunate schisms in Arab ranks. In referring to the current weakening of Arab unity, I speak with most anxious concern, not in criticism, far less in derision. If Arab unity cannot be held and reasserted even in view of the Israeli menace, the prospects would darken for the entire Third World and for equilibrium and peace. In sum, the Middle East offers portents of a situation to which imaginative approaches need to be made.

East Asia in the post-Vietnam war era is another stage for the operation of forces that can bring about a radical overhaul, sooner or later. Apart from the emergence there of a third Communist power, there are other latencies which cannot be confined to any specific area in that vast region south of China and Japan. The rippling effect can reach the South-Asian sub-continent.

Africa has yet to achieve an equipoise. The rearguard action of the despicable racist regimes of southern Africa, the nuclear ambitions of the Pretoria regime, the lack or paucity of resources at the disposal of freedom forces, necessitating external intervention, as in Angola, the regrettable disagreements between African governments in relation to situations of common concern, the inability of the African organization to resolve problems between African states similar to the failure of the Arab organization to settle disputes between Arab governments – all these add up to a situation invalidating the glib diagnoses and prognostications of the past.

If we also survey the Latin American scene where regimes are planted that fail to respond to the people's urge and are, therefore, uprooted, we can see how events are rolling from which no nation or group of nations can escape unless it re-evaluates its relations with others and attunes itself to the rhythm of an unprecedented historical situation.

This is not an age which offers black-and-white options. It allows no water-tight moralistic commitments. It permits no inflexible responses. It condones no frozen animosities. It repels static relations. Developments occur every day which illustrate how the more resourceful nations continually readjust their policies in order not to be caught behind by events. Some of these may be of no intrinsic significance but they do illustrate the need felt by states, especially the dynamic ones, to acquire a greater manoeuvreability. A state does not forsake the friendship of another if it preserves a measure of flexibility regarding a third.

5

Considering the changing political and strategic realities, our three countries – Iran, Pakistan and Turkey – would need one day, not too long in the future, to re-examine the validity and relevance of the policies we have so far adopted towards our association. Time will not stand still to our advantage. If we miss the opportunity to mobilize and integrate our resources in order to face contemporary challenges, the world will take no note of either our heritage or our aspirations. Our collective capacities will then remain immobilized and we will have failed to translate the abstract into the concrete, poetry into politics and romance into reality. I venture to say that it would be a gigantic loss, perhaps an irreparable one, not only to us, not only to the other nations with whom we are affiliated but also to the forces of peace and progress in the world. In that event, the logical development will be for every one to frame individual responses to a developing world situation and readjust relations, not to one another, but on the wider plane.

We have been associated in CENTO and RCD. To speak metaphorically, ours has been a chariot drawn by three horses and moving on two wheels. On the political-strategic and economic terrain of the last quarter of the twentieth century, neither of the two wheels can move with speed. Each is ante-diluvian. This is apparent if we examine the intrinsic strength of these organizations.

It is no reflection on any power that CENTO is not, and was not meant to be, an expression of the Iranian–Turkish–Pakistani community. While it no doubt afforded our three governments useful opportunities of contact with one another, the very auspices and motive force of its establishment were rooted in a world situation which has undergone a qualitative change. Its ineffectiveness has been manifest. Twice it failed to respond when a regional member suffered an armed attack. As His Imperial Majesty the Shahanshah of Iran very aptly said, 'Foreign armies crossed international frontiers while CENTO watched.' One of the principal ailments of this organization has been the inability of the non-regional members to comprehend immediately the significance, intensity and long-term effects of regional crises. They tend to interpret the *raison d'être* of regional security arrangements in a way that may not coincide at a given moment with the perceptions of the regional powers directly affected. This is a psychological fact with which it is futile to quarrel. The distance between the respective evaluations of the regional and the non-regional members cannot be covered by a consultative machinery which is slow and cumbersome and, by its very nature, incapable of speedy response in times of grave emergency.

Apart from this structural defect in CENTO, the larger fact remains that when the strategic environment has radically changed, an institution that fails to absorb such change is inevitably fossilized.

The other organizational link between the three countries is provided by RCD. The point is incontestable that an objective appraisal of RCD would reveal that it has abysmally fallen short of expectations. None of the mutations that have taken place in the international scene during the twelve years since the RCD was formed has had an impact on the purposes and programmes of the organization. Instead of being galvanized into action, the RCD remains embedded in an impervious shell. We cannot be inspired by an organization which would list as its foremost achievement its ability to cling to life and the next one its success in publicising and perpetuating its initials. Responsible observers, when informed of our view of the working of RCD, cannot conceal their amazement at the contrast between its performance and the vast potentialities of which it could be a vehicle. What explains this failure? Surely, we cannot blame a skimpy Secretariat. The question that we have to answer is whether we are unitedly and passionately committed to the Region and to Cooperation and to Development. If we are, do we have the political will to demonstrate that commitment and so qualitatively upgrade the organization that it can stand for a Revolution of Common Determination?

6

The profound historical changes of our times call for some re-thinking on both CENTO and RCD. There are issues that will have to be faced, sooner or later. As early as in 1962, Dr Henry Kissinger termed SEATO and CENTO as the products of 'pactitis'. Since this signal, major world developments have shaken the structure of the two alliances. When some funda-mental premises have fallen and new assumptions are taking shape, it would be myopic to visualize a standstill order and to ignore the value of a nimble approach. The dynamism of the world situation, the twists and turns of the detente, the un-hingement of NATO due to its encirclement from within, as it were, a host of imponderables and incalculable factors, indeed the full flow of events – all demand a re-evaluation in the most salutary sense.

This approach can be adopted without impinging on the firmer relationships founded on bilateral agreements or treaties. The sudden abrogation of these commitments would bring disorder where greater order is needed. While, therefore, they require to be steadfastly upheld, it has to be recognized that an underpinning of durable elements can give them far greater strength. Without a wider scope and sweep, such limited mandates do not evoke the respect from others which larger associations and higher objectives inspire. For the necessary appeal to their own peoples as well as to the world at large, Iran, Pakistan and Turkey need to evolve an integrated frame-work of unity. This would be an entirely indigenous system, an organic association which would exert a gravitational pull on other neighbouring countries that share the same faith and the same aspirations and regional objectives.

Such an evolution would not be vulnerable to the objections, nor provoke the suspicions, which could have been anticipated in the past. With the exercise of statesmanship and a perception of necessities, the strains and misunderstandings that existed in inter-state relations in the Near and Middle East region have been replaced by accommodation and cordiality. With this changed equation, the RCD countries are now in a position most propitious for a creative enterprise.

The three countries no longer need a specifically-oriented alliance. Instead of a consultative framework in a limited sphere which is peripheral in the larger context, they need an organization which will be responsive to the multi-dimensional challenge they face and which will ensure the security, stability and progress of the entire region. It is a region where a ripple of disorder may swell into a tidal wave of instability engulfing a much larger area and cutting across more than one continent. Nothing will more stimulate the evolution of new ideas than a recognition of the need for self-reliance. Equally important is the eradication of habits formed over a long period of dependence on outside powers and sources for the fulfilment of our basic needs. The impositions of embargos at critical moments and the uncertainty of supplies in times of dire need have yielded us an instructive experience.

Interdependence is the essential phenomenon of our times. Not even the super powers, with their immense resources, escape the compulsion of entering into multilateral security and economic arrangements. The compulsion presses more closely on a region whose defence is indivisible. Moreover, contemporary economics underlies the need for multi-national organizations of industry. With a population base of 140 million, the association of the three countries can effect economies of scale and launch high-investment industrial undertakings which would be beyond the financial, managerial or technical capacity of an individual country.

Let us not forget that West Europe aims to become a significant focus of power, with the potentiality of being a balancer of the dominations and rivalries of the super powers. It cannot be said that the countries of West Europe have reached a uniform economic standard. But they have not allowed their disparities or their competition to halt their rapid progress towards economic integration and greater co-ordination of political policies.

There is another phenomenon of great significance of which we cannot fail to take note. The group of non-aligned countries now numbers as many as eighty-two. Such a vast group naturally includes heterogeneous elements. Despite this heterogeneity, despite their internal conflicts and confrontations, despite the assemblage being spread over far-flung continents, the group does seek to strike a common denominator and establish an identity of purpose on international problems. What is more worthy of note is that lately this conglomeration is seeking to relate its standpoint directly to questions of security with the idea of forging political and military collaboration and extending it to supporting 'the forces of independence and freedom in each individual country'. If a group as disparate as the non-aligned, and as antithetical to alignment, can venture to conceive of political and quasi-military alliances against those outside the community of non-aligned states, would it be not tragic that our three countries, so contiguous to one another, so free from internecine quarrels, so moved by the same aspirations, should set our sights low and be reluctant to construct a platform on which they can stand together and act in concert in facing the thrusts and crises of the times?

We are going to Izmir tomorrow not to disturb the constellation. The non-aligned states are to meet in Colombo in August. I doubt if they are poised to shake the world either. But it cannot escape notice that this family of the non-aligned came into being, and raised its voice, against military alliances and military adventures. It stood up to tell the world that it was an apostle of peace and its mission was to remove tensions on the international plane. But now some of them are seeking to discuss military assistance to one another as an aligned combination and thinking of going to any part of the world in support of what is termed as the liberation of the oppressed.

This they are prepared to consider outside the scope of the United Nations Charter. Neither the highest legal restraints of the Charter to which they are committed nor the territorial limits imposed by the existence of state frontiers would seem to deter them from spreading out as the policemen of the world. The very elements that claimed to establish a sanctuary from operations of the great powers are now seeking to expand their own interventionist role to great-power dimensions. I do not assume that discussions along these lines at Colombo will not be abortive nor do I regard it likely that a decision of this character will be adopted. It is obvious enough that such a decision will not only be harmful to the interests of the non-aligned states but make a mockery of the concept of non-alignment and destroy its value. But the very fact that some of the non-aligned states are prepared to go to such an extent is important as it shows what radical responses they are making to what they – rightly or wrongly – perceive as challenges which they should meet.

7

Our three countries have a complementarity in resources and skills and a commonly held *weltanschaung* which would be the envy of many other a region. If we, therefore, add a new dimension to the Charter of the RCD in the realization that we cannot separate our destinies and that, in the last analysis, economic collaboration without political and security arrangements is chimerical, we need not fear the reaction to such an association which might have been provoked in the Dullesian era. The systematic consolidation and formalization of our joint will to defend our civilization against all challenges – economic, political, ideological or military – is something different from adventitious arrangements which are apt to create suspicions in others. A cooperative arrangement by us would be non-exclusive in spirit. It would fan no rancours.

It would reflect the vitality of our societies and be nourished by their energies and enthusiasms. As such, it would be respected by other countries, backed by our friends and sustained by the collective will of our peoples.

My perception of this association and the shape it will acquire, as the foregoing makes clear, is not oriented to military terms. It is focussed on the psyche of the contemporary age. If socio-political and psychological factors are not in their proper place, on the chess-board of international politics, no military acquisitions can provide security against the challenges and threats of our times. In the effort to lend a dimension and depth to our association, in the quest for ways to translate platonic levels of relationship into Aristotelian norms, I am swayed by the belief that military preponderance by itself, without the psychological and political pre-requisites, is incapable of attaining an equilibrium that will endure.

Lastly, the abiding thought in my mind is that we in Pakistan have always been moved by the vision of a larger Muslim nationalism in the Iqbalian sense. Such a nationalism is not a negation of national identities and state sovereignties but complementary to them. In the modern age, no nation can be sufficient unto itself. The Muslim nations need one another even more, because of the depredations they have suffered during the last two or three centuries and because their salvation and lasting security lie in their unity. Concrete progress can be made towards that unity through an association of three countries which have an undeniable importance. It is the vision of the larger unity that remains the anchor of my thoughts.

Karachi
19 April 1976

The second Islamic Summit Conference, attended by 37 countries of Asia and Africa, was held in Lahore in February, four months after the Arab-Israeli war of 1973.

The Conference was sponsored by Pakistan and Saudi Arabia, and though the immediate issue was that of the Holy City of Jerusalem and the withdrawal of Israeli forces from occupied Arab territory, the Conference addressed itself to the formulation of the role of the Muslim States in a larger global perspective.

The key-note address was delivered by Prime Minister Bhutto as Chairman of the Conference. This Chapter reproduces that address.

THE ROLE OF THE
MUSLIM STATES

This unique assemblage of Monarchs, Presidents and Prime Ministers has gathered at a moment in world affairs which is as critical as it can be creative. Here is a resplendent array of statesmen and leaders, profound in their insight into the issues that will engage us at this Conference. By asking me to preside at it, you have conferred an honour upon me which in reality is a tribute to Pakistan. I am filled with both humility and pride: the humility is personal and the pride national.

By agreeing to meet here, this assembly has honoured also the city of Lahore. This ancient city symbolises not only Pakistan's national struggle but also its abiding solidarity with the Muslim world. Here in Lahore lived that magnificent herald of Islamic renaissance, Muhammad Iqbal, who fathered the idea of Pakistan, who articulated the Muslim's anguish and his hope and whose voice sounded the clarion call of revolt and resurgence.

Also here in Lahore, 34 years ago, was adopted the celebrated resolution that inaugurated the glorious freedom struggle of the Muslims of the South Asian subcontinent under the leadership of Quaid-i-Azam Muhammad Ali Jinnah. It is a fact of no small significance that the same session of the Muslim League which adopted the Pakistan resolution also adopted unanimously a resolution on Palestine. The resolution recorded, and I quote, 'the considered opinion, in clear and unequivocal language, that no arrangements of a piecemeal character should be made in Palestine which are contrary in spirit and opposed to the pledges given to the Muslim world'. The resolution further warned against the danger of using force in the Holy Land 'to overawe the Arabs . . . into submission'.

With only the amendments necessary because of the disappearance of British colonialism, the resolution is as pertinent today as it was in 1940. Not the quirks of history but the sublime logic of Providence has decreed that the same warning should again issue from Lahore.

Pakistan's support for the just causes of the Muslim world is organically related to its own national vocation. It has never suffered a severance between its national impulse and the urges of Muslim emancipation. When the partition of Palestine was decided under the British Mandate, a demonstration was held here in Lahore at which Iqbal was present. On that occasion, he emphasized that the problem of Palestine, and I quote his words, 'does not concern Palestine alone but will have wide repercussions in the entire Islamic world'. Later, in October 1947, soon after our emergence, the Quaid-i-Azam warned that the partition of Palestine would entail, and I quote his words, 'the gravest danger and unprecedented conflict' and that 'the entire Muslim world will revolt against such a decision which cannot be supported historically, politically and morally'. Soon afterwards, Pakistan said at the United Nations that the Holy Land was being nailed and stretched on the cross. All these words went unheeded but today, decades later, they are still timely.

Pakistan's involvement with the issue whose scene is the Arab Middle East is accompanied by its deep attachment to its dear neighbour Iran and to Turkey and by friendship and cordiality with other Muslim countries – and if I specially mention Indonesia and Malaysia, I do not underrate our relations with others. Pakistan's cultural history bears a Persian-Turkish stamp. It is an immense source of satisfaction to us that this historical affinity is now reflected in close fraternal relations with both these countries, relations which have proved sustaining in times of stress. With Afghanistan, Pakistan shares a good part of its history, culture and traditions. Pakistan's approach to the problems of the Muslim world is, therefore, informed with a certain range of sympathy and awareness. This, we believe, is in accord with the great ends of Muslim brotherhood.

A few moments ago, in deference to the sentiments of the leaders participating in this Conference and as a result of the mediatory efforts of this Conference, my Government has extended formal recognition to Bangladesh. We hope this mutual reconciliation, which is in the spirit of Islamic fraternity, will now bury a past that the peoples of both our countries would prefer to see forgotten.

2

It is only natural that the leaders of the Muslim world, even when coming to this meeting, should have their minds full of a variety of concerns – some national, others regional, all bearing on Muslim interests. But this Conference cannot address itself except to the specific purpose for which it has been convened as a sequel to the war of October 1973. All of us are aware that the previous Summit Conference, which was held in Rabat in 1969, was convened to consider the question of Jerusalem following the outrage committed under Israeli occupation to the Holy Al-Aqsa Mosque. Likewise, this Conference has a circumscribed agenda. By adopting the agenda, we do not deny that there are other vital issues which agitate Muslim minds. These are burning issues too. Your host country, for instance, has been a victim of international conspiracies and is concerned with an intense question in which, it believes, its stand is based on nothing but justice and concern for Muslim rights. However, we would be doing a disservice to the Conference if we sought to exploit this platform to ventilate our national standpoints. If Muslims sustain their unity, if they mutually strengthen themselves, if they place equity above expedience, if they perceive the direction of historic forces, a time will come when such issues can be discussed without apology or awkwardness. At present, this Conference is primarily concerned with the preeminent issues that are inscribed on its agenda and that concern the heartland of Muslim life and culture.

The situation in the Middle East is an outgrowth of the problem of Palestine and the core of the problem, viewed both historically and concentrically, is Al-Quds or Jerusalem. Fifty years ago, there was no Palestine problem; there was only a country named Palestine. Only the right arrogated to itself by Western colonialism enabled one Western nation to promise to a section of another people, namely the Jews, the country of a third, the Arabs. It needs to be reiterated that it is this fundamental injustice, this uprooting of a people from their homeland and the planting of an alien population on it, that evokes the resentment of the entire Muslim world. The malady consists of a cancerous outgrowth of colonialism, the establishment of settler regimes or the imposition of immigrant minority rule. The root cause of the conflict is not an innate animosity between the Muslim and the Jew or even between the Arab and the Jew. As Muslims, we entertain no hostility against any human community; when we say this, we do not exclude the Jewish people. To Jews as Jews we bear no malice; to Jews as Zionists, intoxicated with their militarism and reeking with technological arrogance, we refuse to be hospitable. The pogroms inflicted on them during the centuries and the holocaust to which they were subjected under Nazism fill some of the darkest pages of human history. But redemption should have come from the Western world and not have been exacted, as it was, from the Palestinians.

The tragedy of Palestine has agitated Muslim minds for half a century. The outrage of its partition in 1947 and the graver injury of its occupation by Israel in 1967 have been intolerable because the territory is part of the spiritual centre of the Muslim world. The Palestine question was referred to the world organization at a time when that organization was hardly representative of the international community. The plan which it put forward for the partition of Palestine would not obtain a passing consideration today from the majority of its membership, consisting of the Third World nations that are sworn to the principle of the self-determination of peoples. Even at that time, the Muslim nations reminded the Western world of its own long-term interests and of the folly of forcibly driving a wedge into the Middle East. These reminders proved fruitless. These importunities were scorned.

This is the historic dimension of the Middle East problem which cannot be banished from sight even when present realities are to be focussed upon. Israel has gorged and fattened on the West's sympathies, nurtured itself on violence and expanded through aggression. It has brought suffering to the inhabitants of the land which it usurped, sequestrated their patrimony and ejected them by the hundreds of thousands. Its neighbouring nations have been robbed of their peace and tranquillity. Its apologists have sought to justify its repeated resorts to force on the ground of security. But nothing could be clearer than that belligerency towards its neighbours will only turn Israel into an international ghetto. Force cannot bring it security nor obduracy peace.

After 1967 Israel became more and more arrogant; it derided the censure of its actions by the United Nations. Its advocates became increasingly apathetic to the growing signs of the untenability of the situation arising from the war of 1967. The result was that an iniquitous, indeed an absurd, situation was frozen and the forces of sanity became immobile.

This was the cause of the war of 1973. A recourse to war can never be a happy decision. Which nation would willingly sacrifice the flowers of its manhood or wish to forfeit its development and mortgage its progress? But situations arise in which there is no choice but war against the usurper. Such a situation was created for the Arab peoples. Tribute is due to them for meeting it manfully. Let us pay homage to those who laid down their lives in the sands of Sinai and the heights of Golan. These martyrs died in the cause of justice and human dignity.

The war has released currents which could flow towards a just settlement of the Middle East problem. The Arab cause has been actively supported by a vast segment of humanity. The nations of Africa have demonstrated their solidarity with Arabs and placed principle above expediency. Under the pressure of the economic forces, if not through a perception of the rights and wrongs of the situation, the Western powers have awakened to the urgency of a definitive settlement of the Middle East problem. The mediatory processes which have thus been put into motion are not to be disdained.

These are good auguries. But they can vanish if an apathy towards the root of the problem, and a satisfaction at partial solutions, begins to sway the policies of those who have supported Israel. On their part, the Arab states have shown that their approach to the problem is not theological, like Israel's, but one which visualizes a series of peaceful adjustments beginning with disengagment.

Disengagement, however, is not peace. It can turn peace into a mirage if it operates as a substitute for a comprehensive settlement. We have a right to expect that the peace which is negotiated in Geneva will deal with all the issues integral to the Middle East conflict. The withdrawal of Israeli forces from all Arab territories occupied since 1967, the restoration of the Holy City to Arab sovereignty and the restitution of the rights of the Palestinian people are the essential elements of a settlement.

All these elements derive from the rational principles of a just and durable peace. All of them come within the four corners of Resolution 242, if that resolution is rightly interpreted. The exponents of the Israeli view contend that the Security Council resolution envisages the possibility of Israel retaining a part of the occupied Arab territories. This contention is sought to be based on the provision regarding the right of every state in the region 'to live in peace within secure and recognised boundaries'. The perversity of such an interpretation is evident from the fact that the resolution as a whole states its objective to be 'the fulfilment of Charter principles'. What principle is more basic to the Charter of the United Nations than the inadmissibility of the acquisition of territory by the use of force? Furthermore, no state can arrogate to itself the right to determine its secure borders even if these encroach on the territory of another. No state claims such a right. The security of a state's frontiers depends on their conformity to international law. A nation's defence strategy is based on its recognised frontiers and not on its aggressive appetites. Finally, the question arises: Whose security comes first? Certainly, on the record of the aggressions committed during the last twenty-seven years, it is the Arabs who need secure borders against Israel and not Israel against the Arabs.

3

Among the Arab territories occupied by Israel, Al-Quds holds a special place in Muslim hearts. A unique symbol of the confluence of Islam with the sacred tradition of Abraham, Moses and Jesus, all of them Prophets whom Muslims hold in the highest reverence, Jersualem is inscribed on our souls as the site of, in the words of the Holy Quran, 'the Farther Mosque the precincts of which Allah has blessed'. Associated as it is with the Ascension of the Last Prophet, it is tied to our inmost spiritual fibre. Except for an interval during the Crusades, it has been a Muslim city – I repeat, a Muslim City – from the year 637

AD. For more than 1300 years, Muslims have held Jerusalem as a trust for all who venerated it. Muslims alone could be its loving and impartial custodians for the simple reason that Muslims alone believe in all the three prophetic traditions rooted in Jerusalem.

We gladly recognise that Jerusalem affects the cherished sensibilities of men and women of three world faiths. But there are two thousand million Muslims and Christians, and fifteen million Jews, in the world. Out of these, less than three million owe their allegiance to Israel. What principle of justice would confer on this minority the right to hold dominion over the Holy City? What except a kind of cynicism can allow the City of Peace to be treated by Israel as the spoils of war?

I must make it clear that it is not *our* position on Jerusalem but *Israel's* which is contrary to the objective criteria by which the status of territories is determined. It is Israel which cites the name of a religion and a culture and invokes its memories or emotions in order to lend justification to acts that are wholly illegal. Such attempts can only make a conflict implacable and bring in its train a religious war. Viewed in a non-religious perspective, the question of Jerusalem's status cannot be unrelated to the sovereign rights of the people of Jerusalem itself, the majority of whom were Arabs, violently expelled and uprooted from the western part in 1948. Nor can the special attachment of Jewish people to Jerusalem override the principle of the inadmissibility of territorial acquisition by force. The Jewish right to Jerusalem certainly connotes the right of access and worship. We cannot recognize any additional right.

On the basis of all these considerations, the issue of the Holy City of Jerusalem admits of no doubt or division in our ranks. Let me make it clear from this platform that any agreement, any protocol, any understanding which postulates the continuance of Israeli occupation of the Holy City or the transfer of the Holy City to any non-Muslim or non-Arab sovereignty will not be worth the paper it is written on.

This is not a threat. I am saying it in full awareness of the intricacies of the negotiations which may be under way. Not to give this warning would be to encourage an illusion which will be fatal to the establishment of lasting peace in the Middle East. In this respect, there is a fire in our hearts which no prevarication, no skilful evasions on the part of others, will ever be able to quench.

The international community, and particularly those states which sponsored the partition of Palestine in 1947, bear a heavy responsibility. They have to redress the injustices perpetrated on the Palestinian people. If it were not also tragic, what could be more bizarre than the phenomenon of a People being dispossessed of its homeland and condemned to live in agony and dispersion, not in imperialism's hoary past but in our day and age? Who cannot understand their anger at seeing immigrants from all over the world invited, nay cajoled, to settle on their own homeland? It is not the eruptions of insensate violence, disowned by their leadership, but the purity of their rights which must influence the world's attitude to their problem.

The states gathered here today are committed by the very fact of their adherence to the Charter of the Islamic Conference to strive for the restitution of the legitimate rights of the Palestinian people. This is our obligation not only to the people of Palestine, not even merely to the cause of Islamic brotherhood, but also to the larger cause of universal peace. We see glimmers today of a new recognition of the need to resolve the problem of Palestine. This recognition has been earned by the heroic sons and daughters of Palestine through their suffering, their fortitude and the constancy of their commitment.

4

We are emerging today out of nearly a half millennium of decline. During this long period, our collective attitude has been one of nostalgia for a vanished glory mixed with an incomprehension of the movements of history. There were occasional thrusts of hope and endeavour but, by and large, we have lived, as Iqbal said, 'in a prison-house of thoughts and emotions which, during the course of centuries, we have forged around ourselves'. 'The superb idealism of our faith,' in Iqbal's words, was stifled by the mediaeval fancies of theologians and legists'. An intellectual lethargy paralysed our thought.Empiricism withered among us. Obscurantism took hold. The spirit of inquiry and enterprise was deadened. Form became more important than substance. We broke ourselves into schisms; we became a collection of warring factions. This brought about the inroads, and eventually the invasion, of Western colonialism. From Maghreb to Indonesia, the Muslim peoples came under the domination, in one form or another, of Western Europe. Our cultures were fragmented, our traditions ruptured and our mutual communications disrupted. The imperialist powers belittled our heritage, pillaged our treasures, denuded us of our resources and the flower of our manhood was sacrificed to serve their strategies. Muslim was turned against Muslim, brother against brother. There was a continuity of setbacks, a succession of disasters, which we shared in common with all the oppressed people of the world.

Not until the Second World War exhausted the warring states of Europe did the era of colonialism come to an end and the nations of the Third World, including the Muslim countries, achieve independence. But mere political independence brought nothing more than the trappings of sovereignty. Economic life in the developing countries remained tied to the so-called 'metropolitan' areas. The Third World remained consigned to the role of supplying raw materials for the industrialized nations. It had no control over the exploitation of its natural resources and no power to determine the prices of the commodities which it produced. Steadily, the value of these commodities fell in relation to the price of industrial goods and services supplied by the affluent nations. This enormous iniquity has been much talked about. The Third World has emphasized, time and again, that poverty and affluence cannot co-exist in the world of today. But apart from the scant response from the industrialized world, we ourselves have not fully realized the nature and value of economic power nor grasped the urgent need of developing science and technology for our progress, indeed for our very survival. We have not appreciated that it was not a want of spiritual strength in us, compared with other peoples, that made humiliation our lot but the weakness of our economic enterprise and organization. After all, even in the darkest days of colonialism, we did not lack faith but we certainly lacked an understanding of economic forces and technology and the role played by them in fashioning a people's fate.

The war of last October has, however, precipitated a chain of events and created an environment in which the developing countries can at last hope to secure the establishment of a more equitable economic order. Some far-reaching possibilities have been opened by the demonstrated ability of the oil-producing countries to concert their policies and determine the price of their resources. This may well be a watershed in history. It may well presage the end of a deranged world order.

With the recent dramatic improvement in the terms of trade of the oil-producing countries, which will lead to a rapid increase in their financial resources, an unprecedented shift will occur in the global monetary and financial balance of power. The Third World can now participate in the economic and financial councils of the world on an equal footing with the developed countries and will be able to acquire a due measure of influence and control in international financial and economic institutions. Indeed, for the first time, the Third World is potentially in a position to use its own resources for financing its development through cooperative effort. It can now forge its own financial institutions for bringing about rapid development of the less developed countries.

These are exciting opportunities. They can be grasped or

they can be missed. For there are also perils and pitfalls in the present situation. The gravest of these is that of a division between the oil-producing and the non-oil-producing countries of the Third World. The dislocation in the balance of payments position of developing countries which has occurred suddenly can be used to sow discord and cause disarray in the ranks of Asian and African nations with grave damage to the political causes they are espousing today.

This is a danger which must be overcome by positive action. Concrete measures have to be evolved, institutions established and machineries devised, which would channel the resources now commanded by the oil producers in such a way as to release them from their dependence on countries outside the Third World for their basic needs and services and also strengthen the Third World economically. The concept implicit in this approach is not that of aid as a form of charity from one developing country to another. The concept is that of mutually supportive economic activity in countries of the Third World which would complement their individual resources and give them a collective economic strength.

I said before that, compared to other peoples, it is not spiritual but economic strength that we have lacked so far. There is no power without economic strength. Unless we reorientate our outlook and try to develop the potential to meet our basic economic and security needs through cooperative endeavour, we will continue to lack the inherent strength, the solidity, which is necessary for achieving our social, cultural and political purposes. The Muslim countries are now so placed as to be able to play a most constructive and rewarding role for cooperation among themselves and with other countries of the Third World. Not only are they possessed of a common heritage and outlook but also their economies are such as to enable them to supplement one another's development effort. It is time that we translate the sentiments of Islamic unity into concrete measures of cooperation and mutual benefit. It will bring us strength in spirit and substance. Let not posterity say that we were presented with an historic, possibly unrepeatable, opportunity to release ourselves from the injustices inflicted on us for many centuries and we proved ourselves unequal to it.

The kind of action that we envisage may entail some new departures. But it can be fuelled by certain positive elements. There are distinct signs of a new vision today. Moved by it, and despite the current hardships they face, the non-oil-producing countries like Pakistan are determined not to succumb to any pressures which would disrupt the unity of the Third World. Efforts are being made to achieve viable solutions in the larger context of the problem of commodity prices in relation to the prices of industrial products. The United Nations certainly has to shoulder a responsibility in this field. We have warmly supported the initiative taken by Algeria to have the problem discussed in a global, and not a parochial, perspective. The issues, though seemingly economic, are political in the deepest sense. But given an attitude of mutual understanding and accommodation, the apparently conflicting interests of the various groups of countries can be reconciled. We must all pool our endeavours towards that objective.

5

As we meet here today, I find it necessary that we should clearly set forth not only our attitudes to the issues of the day but also the bases of Muslim unity. There are certain features of our aim and purpose which are not yet clearly perceived by the rest of the world. These must be stressed if an understanding of the Muslim world is to be promoted in the rest of the human race.

First, we repudiate chauvinism as much as we reject alien dominance. This repudiation arises not only from our recognition of the realities of time and space but from the very spirit and temper of Islam. As there is an arrogance of power, so also can there be an arrogance of belief. Our religion warns us severely against any conceit which would breed the delusion that we are the chosen people and we enjoy an immunity from the operation of the forces that shape the destinies of mankind.

Secondly, our vocation as Muslims is not to harbour hostility against other human communities, East or West, North or South, but to so conduct ourselves that we can help build bridges of communication and sympathy between one set of nations and another. We draw our inspiration from the Holy Quran and I quote:

> 'Say: To Allah belong both East and West: He guideth whom He will to a straight path. Thus we have appointed you a midmost nation that you might be witnesses over the nations and the Apostle a witness over yourselves.'

In being called the midmost nation or the People of the Middle, we are charged with the mission of mediating conflicts, spurning the doctrines of bigotry and hate, trampling underfoot the myths of racial or cultural superiority and translating into social terms the concepts of mercy and beneficence which constitute the core of our faith.

The concept of the People of the Middle is suggestive also of a new synthesis. Through a conventional opposition, the East has been considered as spiritual and contemplative and the West materialistic and pragmatic. Islam rejects such dichotomies. The Muslim accepts both worlds, the spiritual and the material. What he tries to do is to find the reserves of spirituality, the respect for human personality and the sense of what is sacred in all cultural traditions, which could serve to fashion a new type of man. His aim is more than the mere mastery of nature. If he is a true Muslim, he is at once Eastern and Western, materialistic and spiritual, a man of enterprise as well as of grace.

Thirdly, it is inherent in our purpose that we promote, rather than subvert, the solidarity of the Third World. This solidarity is based on human and not on ethnic factors. The distinctions of race are anathema to Islam but a kinship of suffering and struggle appeals to a religion which has always battled against oppression and sought to establish justice. This solidarity reflects the similarity of the historic experiences of the peoples of Asia, Africa and Latin America. They have suffered the same injustices, borne the same travail and are engaged in the same struggle. Theirs is a solidarity of the forces that seek to combat exploitation, end the disparities in mankind's lot and reclaim the inheritance of its majority.

It may well be that, in the cause of the Third World, and in humanity's struggle towards a balanced world order, we, the Muslims, are now being called upon to play a central role.

I must, in this context, refer to a certain ambivalence in our Muslim minds about the role of nationalism in Islam and its compatibility with the establishment of an Islamic community. Let us face it that there has been some uncertainty on this issue. We have several nationalisms among us, Arab and non-Arab, all equally vigorous and vibrant with aspiration. All these nationalisms constitute our responses to the historic situation that we have confronted in our different geographical locations. Nationalism as the motive force of a people's liberation, nationalism as an agent of a people's consolidation, nationalism as a propeller of social and economic progress is a powerful force which we will do nothing to weaken. Furthermore, nationalism is a necessary tributary to the broad stream of human culture. It takes a full understanding of one's own country, of its history and language and traditions to develop an understanding of other countries, of their inner life and of our relations with them. Islam provides both the spirit and the technique of such a mutuality. Patriotism and loyalty to Islam can thus be fused into a transcedent harmony. As Muslims, we can rise higher than our nationalism, without damaging or destroying it.

But we have studied the history of Europe and we cannot refuse to profit from its experience. Nationalism as a breeder of discord and as an agent of untrammelled egoism has brought untold sorrow to the Western peoples. It has limited mankind's horizons, constricted its sympathies. It has spawned wars. Its history is soaked in blood. Not we, the Muslims, alone, but all peoples of the Third World must despise that kind of nationalism. Without, therefore, visualizing the establishment of a supra-national entity which would stifle the positive aspects of nationalism, our grouping together can have no meaning if it does not help us to avoid the perils to which Europe laid prone for nearly four hundred years. It is inevitable that, in the course of human events, we, as nation-states, will sometimes have differences between ourselves. Nothing would be more chimerical than the notion that such differences can be eliminated overnight. But the important thing is our resolve that we shall not let these differences ever be so magnified as to impel one Muslim nation to go to war with another or interfere in its internal affairs.

In an age when no nation can sustain its insularity, at a time when communications and economic forces are serving to promote larger groupings of nations and countries, we owe no apology for the reassertion of the common affinities amongst the countries of the Muslim world.

6

I have ventured to set forth some basic viewpoints of the Islamic Community which, I believe, are beyond controversy among us. As we proceed to our discussions, we have to bear in mind that it would be unrealistic to expect a complete identity of approach and emphasis among thirty-six sovereign states. Each state represented here works under compulsions which cannot be precisely the same as those felt by another. But while we can differ on points of stress and on tactics, I believe we will all hold fast to a unity of purpose and aim. We can say without exaggeration that our purpose is unsullied by any thoughts of aggrandizement. We can say with confidence that our aim is to promote justice and equilibrium. Our unity is not directed against any creed, religious or secular. It is not nourished by hate or rancour. Its drive and force is a passion for justice.

This Conference must awaken the world's appreciation of the fact that the Arab cause is the cause of all countries, small and large, which oppose aggression and will not suffer the use of force to be rewarded with territorial gains.

This Conference must drive home to the world that the cause of the people of Palestine is the cause of all those who believe in the right of a people to determine its own destiny.

This Conference must indelibly impress, indeed brand, on the consciousness of humanity that we will not permit the spiritual vocation of Jerusalem to be subjected to the fortunes of war.

This Conference must herald the coming of an era of fruitful economic cooperation among the developing countries for their common benefit.

Thus, this Conference will contribute towards a covenant of peace in the tormented lands of the Middle East. It will also, I hope, initiate the processes which will result in strengthening the economic, social and cultural enterprises of the Muslim peoples.

7

As I survey this splendid gathering, I recall that as a young student twenty-six years ago, I was asked to address the student body of a University, almost wholly non-Muslim, on the Islamic Heritage. After making a youthful attempt at defining it, I spoke of Muslim unity against exploitation and of Muslim revival and sketched a plan for a Muslim commonwealth. I ventured to predict that a movement in this direction would take shape in the next twenty years.

There have been periods in my life when, like all of us, I have been assailed by doubts whether this vision of mine would be fulfilled. Today, despite all difficulties in our path, I bow my head in gratitude to Allah for making me witness to a scene which should dispel those doubts.

I trust that we will not fritter away the historic opportunities now presented to us. For long centuries, we have hoped for a turning point. That turning point has arrived. The break of a new dawn is not now a forlorn hope. Poverty need no longer be our portion. Humiliation need no longer be our heritage. Ignorance need no longer be the emblem of our identity.

I cannot conclude better than with that sublime prayerful message which comes at the end of the longest chapter of the Holy Scripture:

'Allah tasketh not a soul beyond its scope;

'For it, that which it hath earned and against it that which it hath deserved;

'Our Lord! Condemn us not if we forget or fall into error;

'Our Lord! Lay not on us such a burden as Thou didst lay upon those before us;

'Our Lord! Impose not on us a burden greater than we have the strength to bear;

'Absolve us and forgive us and have mercy on us;

'Thou art our Protector; Grant us succour against those who reject Thee.'

This is the text of an interview published in the Spectator *between the Prime Minister of Pakistan, Zulfikar Ali Bhutto, and George Hutchinson, Deputy Editor of the* Spectator.

Prime Minister Zulfikar Ali Bhutto does not believe in parrying questions. His replies are forthright and he is open with foreign correspondents. The quality of his leadership is as impressive as the range of his knowledge of national and international affairs.

PAKISTAN AND THE
WORLD

Q: Since the death of Chou En-lai the political situation in China has undergone a considerable change. You have displayed a deep understanding of the People's Republic. What is your assessment of the future, not least in relation to Pakistan?

A: Premier Chou En-lai's departure from the scene was a grievous loss to China and, indeed, to Asia and the world. But the view he articulated of the international situation and the broad principles of China's foreign policy was based on Chairman Mao Tse-tung's revolutionary line in external affairs and so acclaimed in China itself. I find no warrant for the view that these principles will now be altered. China's identification with the Third World and its support of the just causes of the exploited and the disadvantaged nations have roots far deeper than the personal realisations of individuals, no matter how eminent. It is a world-view which is organic to the present historical situation. Of course, there might occur some marginal adjustments, as there do in the external relationships of all states, especially those with larger responsibilities – but these will be responses to the dynamics of international life. I doubt whether they will indicate any change in orientation.

My assessment of the future of Pakistan–China relations derives from the fact that these relations are not, and never have been, based on changing expediencies. It was not a fortuitous set of circumstances but a natural recognition of geo-strategic realities that helped their establishment. The sentiments of mutual support and sympathy, flowing from certain shared principles, have infused warmth and cordiality into the relationship. The policy of bilateralism that we follow insulates this friendship from any warping pressures.

2

Q: Many in the West are perturbed by what they see as the ambiguity or obscurity of Soviet foreign policy. They are not sure whether or not the Russians really believe in détente. Have you detected any appreciable changes in the Soviet policy?

A: I do not suppose that, as conceived by their framers, Soviet policies are either ambiguous or obscure. The problem to which you refer is really of a difference of perception. It sometimes reminds me of the fable of the elephant and the six blind men.

I have said it before that détente conjointly incorporates the three elements of cooperation, competition and conflict. Each element comes to the surface as appropriate in a given situation. But 'given situation' does not here mean the objective situation; it means the situation as interpreted by either of the two super-powers. Détente is a complex phenomenon; if you ignore its complexity, you oscillate between an unstudied stance, on the one extreme, and disenchantment, on the other.

Insofar as détente implies the avoidance of conflict, to criticise it would be to castigate virtue. But, insofar as it is less immaculate, it cannot dispel anxieties about global peace. The mutually exclusive expectations from détente were apparent at Helsinki, even during the champagne celebrations of the Final Act. Subsequent events have further underlined this divergence of purposes. To refer to these facts implies no animadversion.

We assume the prevalence of détente in Europe and we will keenly observe its future course. But we would not wish détente to operate in such a way as to cause global or regional imbalances and generate new sources of tension. There is a potentiality here which can be perceived from the considerable pressure on us in this part of the world. It demands watchful diplomacy and a cool-headed assessment of developments and their linkage. Pakistan maintains good relations with the Soviet Union and we would not wish them to be disrupted. Here again, we adhere to the principle of bilateralism that friendship towards one great power entails no unfriendliness towards another.

3

Q : How would you describe the evolution of Pakistan's relations with the West since the events of 1971? Are they altogether to your satisfaction?

A: In 1971, Pakistan was painted in fairly dark colours to public opinion in the West. It was not understood that the unhappy chapter was written by a tripartite congruence of a benighted clique that ruled the country, a frenetic leadership in East Pakistan and an international conspiracy. The voice of reason or realism was barely audible through a crescendo of condemnation. Now that we recollect that scene in tranquillity, with unclouded judgement, it seems incredible that an effectively orchestrated propaganda should have taken in so many men of discernment, some of them shaping the policies of their governments. Events, and not words, puncture myths. The whole subsequent development of both Pakistan and Bangladesh has demolished the assumptions which were then regarded as exciting or poignant discoveries and which caused a stark hostility towards Pakistan. The organic affinity between Pakistan and Bangladesh, regardless of regimes or international manipulation, is a vital element in the composition of the South

97

Asian scene. Only the purblind would now ignore this reality.

In this clearer perspective, our relations with the West have returned to their natural level. There is free reciprocal communication now and we would not wish these channels to be blocked by misunderstandings. Given our geo-political situation, however, it is inevitable that our evaluations will not always coincide with those prevailing in the West. But the important thing is to foster a creative relationship, an unhampered interchange, between Pakistan and the West. My visits to Western capitals have fortified my belief that the endeavour is not unilateral.

Our relations with the United States are buttressed by a number of treaties, bilateral or multilateral, and, on the whole, have proved strong enough to stand the test of time. There were cracks in the structure in the middle 'sixties but these have been repaired by a changed world situation. The edifice serves as a bulwark for peace and stability in our region. In our view, the relationship has matured, rather than weakened, through the readjustments that had to be made because of new international power equations. Parenthetically, I would say that when the United States government took a principled stand in denouncing armed aggression on Pakistan in 1971, it did not 'tilt' towards Pakistan but acted correctly in accordance with the United Nations Charter. Subsequent events have vindicated that American attitude. In 1973, during my visit to Washington, the United States government categorically stated that the independence and integrity of Pakistan was a cornerstone of the American foreign policy. In 1975, the United States decided to lift a most anomalous, ten-year-old arms embargo. But this will not, as some might insinuate, result in an unrestricted flow of arms to Pakistan. Our financial constraints and the obstructing conditions imposed by the US Congress continue to hamper our effort to fulfil our country's essential defence requirements.

The evolution of Pakistan's relations with the West hinges

on three factors: geostrategic, cultural and economic. The first arises from Pakistan's occupying an important position relating to the Persian Gulf by virtue of its proximity to the oil-producing states and its special relations with Iran. Equipped with credible defence, Pakistan can significantly contribute to the promotion of stability in this vital oil-bearing region. A weakened Pakistan, on the contrary, would portend disorder in this whole area, with repercussions far beyond this region. The cultural factor arises from our appetite for Western learning and technology. English is still our official language. Even when it ceases to be so, it will remain our passport for Western scholarship and science; we will want more rather than less of it. This, of course, presupposes ungrudging cooperation from the other side. Should we be denied access to technology, for instance the nuclear technology that we need urgently to overcome the problem caused by the paucity of indigenous fuels, there will be a considerable reaction; an erosion of our current intellectual rapport with the West will be an immediate consequence. The third factor, the economic one, is at present the most pressing.

The European Common Market is Pakistan's largest trading partner. One indication of our growing relationship with it is the recently concluded agreement for commercial cooperation. The larger question, however, is that of promoting a cooperative dialogue on economic relations between the West and the Third World which would be to the lasting benefit of each side. To be candid, the signs so far have been most discouraging – witness the dismal outcome of the Fourth UNCTAD and the statements at the Paris Conference. To rescue this dialogue from incoherence and fragmentation, I have proposed a conference to the Third World leaders to meet and devise a strategy for an equitable economic order in the world. I doubt whether lesser expedients will constitute an adequate response to the present historical situation.

4

Q: In your estimation, is it practical or realistic to speak of an Islamic bloc in world politics, given the divisions or differences between some of the Muslim states?

A: The divisions or differences between some of the Muslim states are but the after-effects of the operation of colonialism for more than a century. The historical fact is that most of the Muslim countries had been either directly subjugated or subjected to enormous colonial pressures. It is only for two or three decades – in some cases, less – that they have enjoyed a freedom from alien domination. During this time, they have all been engaged, each in its own way, in consolidating their independence. This is too brief a span of time, especially in an unsettling and turbulent age like ours, for the concept and the living sentiment of Islamic fraternity also to find a cohesive expression in the workings of world politics. Yet the very establishment of the Islamic Conference is by itself significant. The Muslim nations constitute one-fifth of the world's population and occupy one-sixth of its landmass. What except the unity based on a felt and natural affiliation will ensure them a proportionate influence in the making of decisions affecting themselves and the world? No; Muslim unity is not a pipe-dream. It is the direction of the evolution of international affairs in the Muslim world. All distractions notwithstanding, it is the goal that has beckoned the best minds of this world for centuries.

But I must stress that exclusivism is anathema to Islam. Muslim solidarity *per se* can have no racial bias, no permanent antagonism; when it is true to its character, the Islamic community is always outward-looking, never ingrown. If, at the present turning-point in history, the Muslim nations are inextricably linked with the Third World, it is because the Third World's cause is but another name for humanity's struggle towards a more equitable world order.

5

Q: Are the internal conditions now prevailing in India conducive or otherwise to an improvement in Indo-Pakistan relations?

A: Before I deal with your specific question, let me make it clear that Pakistan is determined to help create, as best it can, an environment of peace, security and stability in South Asia. To break the stalemate that had interrupted the process of normalizing relations between Pakistan and India, as envisaged in the Simla Agreement of 1972, I took several initiatives. In December last year, I offered to meet Mrs Gandhi in order to overcome the impasse. When I got no response, I decided in March 1976 to withdraw Pakistan's case against India from the International Civil Aviation Organization. This furnished the necessary impetus. With communications and diplomatic relations restored to the state they were in between 1947 and 1965, there is nothing but the unresolved dispute over the State of Jammu and Kashmir which bars genuine neighbourly relations between the two countries. This is a most important issue which has to be settled sooner or later – the sooner, the better. There exists an agreement, evolved by the United Nations and freely accepted by both India and Pakistan, that the dispute shall be settled in accordance with the wishes of the people of that State. We cannot acquiesce in any abrogation of that agreement. Even if the agreement had not been concluded, the fact would still remain that no settlement can be valid or viable which is not freely accepted by the people involved.

It is my hope that India will perceive the necessity of this settlement to its own long-term interest and to reconciliation in South Asia. I say this without any particular implication as far as India's internal conditions are concerned. Some people delight in pontificating about the internal situation of other countries; I don't. Each country achieves it own equilibrium; the luckier ones without much expense in human freedom and private happiness; the less fortunate after much torment and trial and error. Though Pakistan and India became independent at the same time and with similar replicas of colonial institutions, the political experience of one has run a course totally different from that of the other. India has travelled from a quasi-liberal democracy to whatever the present political system connotes. We moved from political confusion to authoritarianism and from arbitrary rule to democracy. Our experience has been much more costly but it has also been more creative.

How the internal conditions in India will impinge on Pakistan–India relations is an interesting question. I cannot return a dogmatic answer. There are potential ties, both positive and negative. If, in the present situation, the Indian government is less prone to the pressure of those elements in India for whom hatred against Pakistan is the breath of their nostrils and dreams of hegemony their daily bread, if chauvinism is bridled and an ancestral bigotry held in check, then I see a distinct possibility that India will move towards a reconciliation with Pakistan through a just and honourable resolution of the Kashmir dispute. This would involve no exercise in magnanimity; all it would signify would be a healthier perception of the realities of South Asia, primarily India's. Resources could be diverted from the futility of arms acquisition to urgent social and economic needs. We would not witness the unaccountable Indian phenomenon, in the midst of pervasive poverty, of a standing army of a million men, an active nuclear weapons programme and a defence budget of four billion dollars. The consolidation of its political power could provide the present leadership in India with an unprecedented opportunity to take bold but correct decisions relating to Pakistan and, indeed, to the peace and stability of South Asia as a whole.

Of course, there are negative potentialities as well; no responsible government can rule them out and rely on hope alone. If conditions in India deteriorate, Pakistan will take due note of it and frame its responses to the situation as it develops. We take nothing for granted.

6

Q: Are you satisfied with the pace of political progress and the development of the economy in Pakistan since your assumption of power?
A: I loathe a complacent posture. The pace of political progress and economic development can be judged from several vantage-points, depending on the time-frame. In the narrower perspective of four or five years, I can claim that we have made sufficient, indeed rapid, headway. The broken Pakistan of 1971, with its identity splintered and its direction confused, seems like a distant nightmare now. The fact alone testifies to our psychological recovery. The recovery would not have been possible without framing a permanent constitution for the country based on the consent of all parties and all provinces – something that had not been achieved by any previous regime in the country. Nor would it have been speeded had we not founded institutions of representative government and inter-provincial coordination and had we not also focused attention on economic reforms aiming at the eradication of exploitative systems and on development projects which can bring about a qualitative change in our economy. This is cause for gratitude. But in the larger perspective, as you take a longer look, you cannot be satisfied unless you see your vision fulfilled and your dream realized. My vision is that of a Pakistan whose social standards are comparable to those in parts of Europe. This means a war against illiteracy and ignorance. It means fighting prejudice and obscurantism. It involves the equality of men and women. It demands the mobilization of the people's collective energies. It dictates the restoration to the human person, the citizen of Pakistan, of the dignity which is his due. It requires a check on the growth of population and easy access to education and medical care throughout the country. It contemplates better towns and cities and cleaner villages. It poses a hundred challenges. It is a long haul. We have braced ourselves for it.

NOTES ON BILATERALISM

The Chinese People's Republic was proclaimed in Peking on 1 October 1949, after the final defeat of the Chiang Kai-Shek forces by the Chinese Communists. Pakistan was among the first to extend recognition (on 4 January 1950) to the Central People's Government of the People's Republic of China. Accordingly, when the question of Chinese representation in the United Nations was raised at the Session of the General Assembly held that year with India moving a draft resolution that the Central People's Government of the Chinese People's Republic represent China in the United Nations, Pakistan voted in favour of this resolution.

Between 1951 and 1960, the proposition did not come before the General Assembly in this direct form. However, the issue never ceased to command attention. At every annual session, the United States proposed that consideration of the question be deferred.

Consequent on the Korean war, the United States sponsored a draft resolution in 1951 seeking to brand China an aggressor in Korea. Pakistan abstained from voting on it. Likewise in 1952, when the United States sponsored a resolution in the General Assembly calling for postponement of the consideration of the question of China's representation, Pakistan again abstained. But in 1953 the Pakistan delegation to the General Assembly voted *for* the postponement of this question's consideration even though the brief had provided for abstention. In 1954 Pakistan joined SEATO and from then on its attitude on the question of China's representation showed scant regard to the real position in China, to its own recognition of the Chinese Government and to the sentiment of the Asian-African membership. This position continued at successive sessions.

In 1957, Pakistan had at first abstained from voting on the resolution due to certain procedural considerations arising from a slight change in the US resolution. However, following an immediate American *demarche* to the Pakistan delegation, led by the Foreign Minister and including the Foreign Secretary, the delegation changed its vote the next day *in favour* of the resolution blocking China's representation by its legitimate government. It informed the UN Secretary-General that the previous vote had been incorrectly recorded. A reversal of a vote exercised during the Assembly's proceedings and so recorded is a most unusual, indeed a humiliating, act for any delegation. Pakistan did not flinch from such self-abasement on this issue during this phase of its attitude towards the great powers.

On 22 September 1958, at a time of tension between China and the United States over Taiwan, the Chinese Foreign Office addressed a note to the Pakistan Government which, in substance, stated that, on most international issues, Pakistan had sided with America and, while China did not expect a great change in Pakistan's foreign policy, she would like to know the attitude of Pakistan as an Asian nation in the dispute over the status of Taiwan. Instead of giving a forthright answer in accordance with China's rightful claim that Taiwan was an integral part of her territory and on the consideration that not even the Chiang Kai-Shek clique upheld the two-Chinas theory or sought separate recognition as the Government of Taiwan, Pakistan sent a reply on 1 October 1958 asserting that she had given neither *de facto* nor *de jure* recognition to the government in Taiwan and urging that no party should take action that would threaten world as well as regional peace.

The following passage from the reply was particularly disingenuous and meant to cause offence to China: 'The juridical position of sovereignty over Formosa is not clear. The problem should therefore be settled by peaceful negotiations. The wishes of the local inhabitants should be given due consideration.'

The Prime Minister of Pakistan and Begum Liaquat Ali Khan have been invited by the Union of Soviet Socialist Republics to visit Moscow. The invitation has been accepted. It is understood that the invitation was conveyed to Mr Liaquat Ali Khan by the Russian Ambassador in Iran through the Pakistan Ambassador, Mr Ghazanfar Ali Khan, during the Prime Minister's recent visit to Tehran.

The official announcement of the invitation and its acceptance was made by Pakistan's Minister for Foreign Affairs, Chaudhri Mohammad Zafrullah Khan, at a press conference in Karachi on Wednesday evening . . .

Asked if the Prime Minister's visit to Moscow would lead to the establishment of diplomatic relations between Russia and Pakistan, the Foreign Minister pointed out that the two countries had already agreed to exchange diplomatic representatives, but the exchange had not been possible so far on account of 'shortage of personnel' in Pakistan.

Dawn, Karachi, 9 June 1949

'The question is asked: Why don't we (the Muslim countries) get together rather than be tied to a big power like the UK or America? My answer to that is that zero plus zero plus zero is after all equal to zero. We have, therefore, to go farther afield rather than get all the zeros together because they will never be able to produce anything which is substantial.'

From H. S. Suhrawardy's speech at Salimullah Hall, Dacca
Dawn, Karachi, 12 December 1956

At the time of the historic Suez crisis of 1956, Prime Minister Suhrawardy addressed the National Assembly and, in the course of his statement, said:

'Today we see no reason why the United Kingdom, having obeyed the mandate of the United Nations, should not sit with us in order to promote the security of the Middle East and also to strengthen ourselves. We know perfectly well that unfortunately the strength which the Middle East countries possess is not sufficient to guard them either against aggression from any sources or from internecine warfare, and as I said elsewhere, any number of zeros cannot make more than zero, whereas if you add one to it, the larger number of possible zeros the greater will be the ultimate result, whether they are put in front or put in the rear, they are more than zero.'

National Assembly Debate, Vol. 1, 1957: pp 917 and 918

A summary containing some directive principles was submitted to the Cabinet by the Foreign Minister, Mr Manzur Qadir. The Commerce Minister, Mr Z. A. Bhutto, stated that 'the summary created an impression that our foreign policy had been determined by our acceptance of the US aid and the course had already been set. . . The two vital problems for us were the problems of Kashmir and Canal Waters. We had to determine how far our foreign policy had helped us to achieve the solution of these problems. It seemed quite certain that in case of war with India, USA was not going to help us.' 'We should not,' he added, 'unnecessarily extend the principle of attachment to the United States.' The Foreign Minister rejoined that the summary was based 'on an objective appreciation of the circumstances that limited our manoeuvrability in the field of foreign affairs'. The President, Mr Ayub Khan, analysing the country's situation, concluded that 'there was not much room for flexibility in our foreign policy'. He added that 'it was a fact that we needed aid and, therefore, we should not behave in a manner which would annoy those who give us aid for the development and security of our country. The aid given to us by the USA was aimed at helping us maintain our independence in an area which was threatened by communism.'

When the point was raised that 'we should show some flexibility in our attitude towards China and work for its acceptance as a member of the United Nations' the response was that 'any such attempt on our part at the moment would undoubtedly upset the United States Government'. In regard to the Third World, the opinion was expressed that 'it was not really a bloc but a group of countries which were oscillating between the two blocs'.

Another point that was made at the meeting was that 'we should try to develop good relations with India because that would further improve our relations with America'.

At the next meeting on 24 December, the Kashmir issue was considered.

Mr Z. A. Bhutto, Minister for Commerce, emphasized that 'we had to continue to press the Kashmir case' and suggested the alternative of approaching the General Assembly under Article 10 of the Charter because of the Soviet veto in the Security Council. The Secretary-General developed the argument that a reference to the General Assembly would 'exhaust all avenues of agitating our case before the United Nations'. It seemed advisable, therefore, 'to follow the same policy as had been followed in the past'.

The President (Mr Ayub Khan) said that 'it was true that the Baghdad Pact had rendered the solution of Kashmir more difficult but it had underwritten the integrity and security of Pakistan. In a situation of stalemate, the most important thing was to have enormous patience and capaity to wait.'

Among the points made by other participants (without attribution) at the meeting were:

(a) We should not undertake the experiment of leaning towards China.

(b) We should avoid technical aid or cultural cooperation with the Soviet Union and 'be cautious about developing trade relations with Communist countries because the US Government might not approve of the idea'.

(c) When it was urged (presumably by the Minister of Commerce) that trade relations with Socialist countries were important for our cotton, the President stated that 'we should offer our surplus cotton to America for sale and explain to them our predicament. If they were unable to purchase it, we should negotiate with the Communist countries.'

However, it was decided that 'the Ministry of Commerce should review the existing trade arrangements with Communist countries with a view to maximising the export of cotton and other commodities'.

Moscow, May 10: Unsmiling and grim, Premier Khrushchev last night threatened diplomats from Pakistan and Norway that Russia would attack the bases used by foreign planes which violate Soviet frontiers.

The Soviet leader made his threat in a man-to-man talk with diplomats of the two countries at a party held in the Czech Embassy in Moscow.

Premier Khrushchev called Norway's Ambassador, Oakar Gunderson, and Mr Salman Ahmad Ali, Counsellor in the Pakistan Embassy, who was deputising for Pakistan's Ambassador to the Soviet Union, to step before him.

He told them: 'If you continue to let the Americans fly from your air bases into Russia, then we will not only shoot down the US planes but will have to aim our rockets at your bases as well.'

. . . The Premier was quoted as saying that Peshawar had now been marked on a map and a ring made round it by Soviet defence forces.

Despatch by Ross Mark
Dawn, Karachi, 11 May 1960

'Let me assure you that we have the deepest interest in your affairs and we hope you will have the same interest in our affairs because, let me tell you, that if there is real trouble, there is no other country in Asia on whom you will be able to count. The only people who will stand by you are the people of Pakistan.' (Applause)

This is an excerpt from President Ayub Khan's address to the U.S. Congress.

From CONGRESSIONAL RECORD-HOUSE
12 July 1961, page 12396

In 1958 Pakistan's relations with China were under great strain. They deteriorated further in the following year. President Ayub Khan who later claimed to be the architect of friendship with China, had no qualms in criticising both China and the Soviet Union and dwelling again and again on 'the danger from the North'. In 1959, he formulated a scheme for joint defence with India obviously against China and the Soviet Union. On 19 January

1960, he declared: 'I foresee China moving south through Burma and Russia through Afghanistan and Iran, if there is no clash between the two of them . . . These moves need not necessarily be military: ideological penetration with communist-backed regimes would do.' He conveyed to the Indian Prime Minister Nehru that an agreement on joint defence could be achieved through goodwill and understanding on both sides; a formal pact would not be needed. His thesis was that Indian and Pakistani forces which were facing each other should be released to defend against 'aggression from a third party' (meaning China and the Soviet Union). The strategy he had conceived was that of friendship with India to the point of military collaboration and hostility against both China and the Soviet Union on the assumption that, in this way, Pakistan would secure Kashmir and an inflow of increased American assistance. Mr Nehru's response was an apposite commentary on this kind of thinking.

The following are a few of the relevant press reports on this subject:

The President, General Mohammad Ayub Khan, yesterday warned that in five years the Pakistan-Bharat subcontinent would become militarily vulnerable to major invasions from the north.

General Ayub Khan said that the invasions would most probably be directed against the bigger segment of the subcontinent, Bharat, but Pakistan was also in the way. The President was last evening giving *his impressions as a military man* of the recent developments in Tibet and Afghanistan, flanking the subcontinent.

He told a news conference at the President's House that the position could be defended if both Pakistan and Bharat dissolved their differences and ceased to face each other with loaded rifles. *Pakistan, he said, would very much like to defend Bharat in such an event.* (Italics supplied.)

Morning News, Karachi, 24 October 1959

The substance of this statement was reported not only in the Pakistan press but also abroad. The *Times of India* of 24 October 1959, for example, gave it the headlines 'Threat to India and Pakistan: General Ayub Khan calls for unity'.

Tehran, Nov. 9 (Reuter). President Mohammad Ayub Khan of Pakistan was today reported to have said in an interview that Chinese occupation of Tibet and road-building activities in Afghanistan posed a serious threat from the north.

The Tehran newspaper, *Kayhan International*, said that in a Karachi interview the Pakistan President said to its correspondent:

'The subcontinent will be vulnerable to attack within five years. Chinese occupation of Tibet and road construction activities in Afghanistan pose a serious threat from the north. It is a threat that cannot be overlooked by wishful thinking.'

Referring to Indo-Pakistan differences, President Ayub Khan was reported as saying that the canal waters dispute was on its way to being solved.

The Pakistan President also termed the Kashmir settlement as 'a final phase in the overall settlement with India'. He said, 'Should this be accomplished, then the question of mutual defence of the Indian subcontinent could be earnestly entered into.'

Morning News, Karachi, 9 November 1959

Asked to comment on the latest Chinese incursion in Ladakh, he said that *it was India's problem* and he was not in a position to say anything as there were not enough details available. (Italics supplied.)

Dawn, Karachi, 4 November 1959

President Ayub said he would be glad to invite Pandit Jawaharlal Nehru if any opportunity arose. Of Ladakh, he said that *it was India's conern*. (Italics supplied.)

Morning News, Karachi, 4 November 1959

---

11 November 1959

Dear Mr President,

For the past several weeks, I have been anxiously concerned with the India-China situation in Ladakh and the impact it can have on our position regarding Kashmir. I noticed in the press that, during an airport interview, you were asked a question regarding this situation and you replied to the effect that it was India's problem. I do not know what exactly was the wording of your statement and whether it was accurately reported in the press.

However, even taking it as reported, your statement was, of course, correct, both factually and from a military point of view, and I have no doubt that our friends will read it in that light. At the same time, however, it is possible that, on another occasion, India and its friends will construe, and probably use, a statement of this kind in an altogether different sense.

I would go even further and say that, in fact, it is a question not only of the statement we have made but of the entire attitude we are going to evince in the matter. The dangers that lie in our attitude as so far shown can be spelled out as follows:

(a) We can be taken to have tacitly recognized India's authority over that part of Kashmir which she controls at present. After all, it is by virtue of the present partition of Kashmir that India controls Ladakh and is in a position to declare that China's encroachment on Ladakh is an encroachment on India itself.

(b) The present situation can be cited by India as justifying any augmentation of forces that she might effect in Jammu and Kashmir, the contrary provisions of the UNCIP resolution notwithstanding. This augmentation of forces will include any tightening of control over Kashmir, any building of roads and airports and, in fact, any other measures that she might undertake.

(c) We can be deemed to be stopped from saying in future that the responsibility for the preservation of the territory of Jammu and Kashmir is not that of India but of the Security Council. We have so far always taken the stand that Jammu and Kashmir is not Indian territory and, therefore, the question of its external defence is a matter for the Security Council, and the Council alone, to consider. We can now be taken to have virtually abandoned that stand.

In my humble but emphatic opinion, it seems to me that we must make some kind of an authoritative pronouncement which would effectively safeguard us against these dangers. A draft letter to the Security Council, if that is going to be the means of making this pronouncement, is under preparation in the Mission here and will be soon submitted to you.

I can assure you that, in making this suggestion, I am not at all unmindful of the complexity of the present situation and the delicacy of our relationship with China. With as much anxious and careful thought as I am able to give to the matter, I feel that a statement, which clearly declares our stake in Kashmir, will not necessarily embroil us with China. On the contrary, it may even be that China will not react adversely to a statement from Pakistan questioning the very basis of the stand taken by India regarding Ladakh.

As far as the effect of a statement of this kind on India is concerned, we cannot ignore the fact that, in spite of all trends and efforts to the contrary, the Indian Government persists in writing letters to the Security Council about Kashmir which consist of the same pseudo-arguments and fulminations that Krishna Menon has been spouting during the last several years. Regarding the effect on the Canal Waters negotiations, we have, of course, carefully to consider the matter but we cannot let India damage our entire position on Kashmir during the time these negotiations remain pending. The solution seems to be to make a statement, unhostile in tone and confined only to a principle. Such a statement, after all, will not be the first or the only example that we have not achieved that final and definitive settlement of all our disputes with India which the outside world seems to imagine.

I am taking the liberty of making this suggestion to you because, in my consultations here, I have found a great anxiety lest the present India-China situation allows the impression to settle that Pakistan no longer feels itself concerned with Jammu and Kashmir. This, of course, is only one aspect of the matter and it is for you to view it in the larger perspective which will take into account the attitude of the United States. At the present moment, however, this aspect seems to be quite important in itself. I do hope that you will not mind my taking an opportunity to make this suggestion to you.

Yours respectfully,
Zulfikar Ali Bhutto

Field Marshal Mohammad Ayub Khan, HJ, HPk,
President of Pakistan,
Rawalpindi.

11 November 1959

My dear Foreign Minister,

I enclose copy of a letter which I have addressed to the President. I have no doubt that you are aware of all the implications of the question touched upon in the letter and of all the possibilities, both good and evil, which are latent in the present situation.

It is my feeling that we shall have to examine the whole question in depth and not let the India-China situation regarding Kashmir drift and develop to our detriment.

Sincerely yours,
Zulfikar Ali Bhutto

Manzur Qadir, Esq.,
Minister of Foreign Affairs,
Government of Pakistan,
Karachi.

Rawalpindi, Nov. 23. Pakistan would not recognise the creation of a no-man's land in Ladakh as suggested by the Indian Prime Minister, Mr Nehru, to the Chinese Premier, said Field Marshal Mohammad Ayub Khan while replying to questions on his attitude to Mr Nehru's latest proposals to China on Ladakh when he arrived here tonight after a tour of Iran and Turkey.

The President said that *Ladakh was a disputed area* and arrangements suggested by Mr Nehru would not be recognized by Pakistan.

Asked whether he had communicated to the Indian Prime Minister that Pakistan would not recognize any such arrangement, the President replied, 'Let such an arrangement come.' Asked if Pakistan would approach the United Nations on the subject, he said, 'Let time come.' (Italics supplied.)

Dawn, Karachi, 24 November 1959

Rawalpindi, Nov. 23 (APP). The President, Field Marshal Ayub Khan, said here today that Pakistan would not recognize any arrangement between India and China in Ladakh *as the area was a disputed territory between Pakistan and India.*

The President was replying to questions by newsmen at Chaklala aerodrome immediately after his arrival this evening from Karachi by way of Lahore.

He was asked to comment on the Indian Prime Minister's proposal to China for creating a no-man's-land in Ladakh. Asked if he would communicate to the Indian Prime Minister on the subject, he said Pakistan would see what happens in this connection. Let such an arrangement come, then we can talk, he added.

Mr Nehru has proposed to the Chinese Premier in a communication that the area in dispute in Ladakh between India and China, some 8,000 miles, be made a no-man's-land as an interim measure pending a final settlement of the frontier between the two countries in that sector. (Italics supplied.)

Morning News, Karachi, 24 November 1959

Excerpts from letter dated 3 December 1959 addressed to the President of the Security Council.

Under instructions from my Government, I have the honour to draw the attention of the Security Council to reports, widely published in the international press, of recent events in the eastern part of the province of Ladakh of the State of Jammu and Kashmir.

'For reasons which are evident and need no explanation, my Government is not in a position to ascertain the veracity of these reports or to determine the actual extent of the encroachment, if any, by a foreign power into the area in question which is an integral part of the Jammu and Kashmir State. It follows that my Government is not able to endorse, or comment upon, the reasons for action and for counter-action taken by either side in the controversy between India and China and in the confusion which has been attendant upon the events in Ladakh . . .

My Government is bound by its duty to declare before the Security Council that, pending a determination of the future of Kashmir through the will of the people impartially ascertained, no positions taken or adjustments made by either of the parties to the present controversy between India and China, or any similar controversy in the future, shall be valid or affect the status of the territory of Jammu and Kashmir or the imperatives of the demilitarization and self-determination of the State laid down in the resolutions of the United Nations.

My Government regards it as a matter of self-evident principle that it is for the sovereign authority freely evolved by, and acceptable to, the people of Jammu and Kashmir, and for that authority alone, to effect, or refuse to effect, any adjustment of its frontiers with any foreign power and that the emergence of such an authority shall not be allowed to be impeded by any necessity, supposed or real, of military defence felt at present by any party within the territory of Jammu and Kashmir.

> Aly Khan
> Ambassador Extraordinary and Plenipotentiary,
> Permanent Representative of Pakistan to the United Nations

By 1959, the policy of supporting the United States on the issue of denying the People's Republic of China its right immediately to represent the country at the United Nations had acquired the stamp of a tradition. The first move towards a change came in 1960 when the Pakistan delegation was led by Mr Z. A. Bhutto, Minister for Fuel, Power and Natural Resources and it exercised the option to abstain instead of voting for postponement. In accordance with the brief, the Pakistan delegate in the Credentials Committee was authorised, for the first time since 1952, to abstain on the US-sponsored postponement resolution. But the reaction of the United States was again a demarche. As a result, within two days of the vote in the United Nations, the discretion originally given to the leader of the Pakistan delegation was countermanded and he was given new instructions. He emphatically disagreed with them.

When next year the same position was sought to be maintained, the leader of the Pakistan delegation, Mr Bhutto, addressed a telegram to the then Foreign Minister, Mr Manzur Qadir, expressing his disappointment at the Pakistan Government's decision. He followed it with a letter on 14 October to Foreign Minister Manzur Qadir, advocating support for the restoration of China's right in the United Nations and hoping that next year Pakistan's voting would be different.

The following is the text of the letter:

Pakistan Mission to the United Nations
Pakistan House
12 East 65th Street
New York 21, NY
October 14 1960

My dear Foreign Minister,

The General Assembly decided on 8 October 1960, to reject the Soviet request for inclusion in the agenda of the item entitled 'Representation of China in the United Nations', and also ruled out any consideration of the question of seating the representatives of the People's Republic of China during the present session.

The vote in favour of rejection was 42; 34 against and 22 abstentions. Pakistan voted in favour of rejection of the motion to include the item on the agenda, in conformity with your instructions.

When the Assembly first considered the question of Chinese representation in 1950, Pakistan had voted for Peking's admission to the United Nations in consequence of the fact that we had extended recognition to it and also because the existence and consolidation of the Communist regime had by then become a fact of international life. Subsequently, however, we changed our position. Since 1956, we have voted against the inclusion of the item in the agenda.

Over the years, the strength of the United States' position in the Assembly on this item has eroded. Last year, 44 countries were ranged behind the United States, 29 were against and 9 had abstained. This year, the US majority was whittled down to 42 with 34 against and 22 abstentions. The two votes lost were Laos and Malaya, which last year supported the United States. This year, both abstained. Furthermore, Cuba and Ethiopia which abstained last year, voted against the United States at the present session. Of the 17 newly-admitted States (16 African and Cyprus), Mali, Senegal and Nigeria voted against the United States. Not one supported the move for rejecting consideration of the question at the present session. All the others, except Congo (Leopoldville) which was not represented, abstained.

After the Soviet Union succeeds in having the item inscribed on the agenda (the required number of votes may well come from the 22 abstentions this year), a resolution may be introduced to the effect that the General Assembly decides to seat the representatives of the People's Republic of China. It will be argued that this resolution requires a two-thirds majority vote, which the Asian, African and Eastern bloc countries cannot muster. They may, therefore, argue that only a simple majority is required, which they possess. This point will have to be decided by the Assembly. Under the rules of procedure a decision as to whether a resolution requires two-thirds majority vote or not is itself taken by simple majority. Thus Asian, African and East European countries should be able to get a decision that the vote on the resolution will be by simple majority. As they will possess the required number of votes, the motion to seat the Communist Chinese representatives will be carried.

The above is speculative in nature. It is difficult to forecast with accuracy as to whether the procedural fight will take precisely this form.

You will also notice from the voting record which I attach, that the division in the Assembly did not take place on an East-West basis. Two NATO allies, namely Norway and Denmark, voted against the United States. A third, Portugal, abstained. I do not, therefore, see why Pakistan should not be considered a staunch ally, any less than these countries if we take a stand on the merits of the question and a recognition of realities.

My initial instructions to the delegation to abstain had been given with these considerations in mind. It is too late to do anything in the matter this year. I can only hope that it will not be too late next year.

Yours sincerely,
Zulfikar Ali Bhutto

Manzur Qadir, Esquire,
Minister for Foreign Affairs,
Government of Pakistan,
Rawalpindi.

After this, Pakistan recovered its capacity to approach the issue on merit. In 1961, Pakistan voted in favour of the draft resolution to seat the representatives of the People's Republic at the United Nations.

When, a decade later, the representatives of the discredited Chiang Kai-Shek regime were ousted from the world organisation, the procedural course adopted by the General Assembly did not vary much from the one anticipated in this letter.

Following the despatches received from Mr Z. A. Bhutto, Minister of Fuel, Power and Natural Resources, who led the Pakistan Delegation at the 15th Session of the UN General Assembly in 1960, a Summary to the Cabinet was submitted by the Foreign Secretary on 24 October 1960. The following views of Mr Bhutto were quoted in the Summary:

(a) *Chinese Representation at the UN:* 'I feel that the time has come for Pakistan to adopt an attitude in the United Nations more consistent with its recognition of the Peking regime than has been the case since 1954.'

(b) *Our attitude to Afro-Asian Issues:* 'It is imperative that in so far as our vital interests are not adversely affected, we should try to strengthen our position among the Asian-Africans . . . An important and obvious way of doing so would be to alter our stand on the issue of Chinese representation and Portuguese colonies in Africa.'

(c) 'Neutralism is bound to emerge as a political philosophy with a wide appeal and possibly as a third force.'

The then Permanent Representative of Pakistan at the UN had made the following points at variance with Mr Bhutto's views:

(a) 'We cannot re-build our position among Afro-Asians so we should work for splitting that group . . . The Africans voted for Nehru's Resolution blindly, innocently, emotionally.'

(b) 'We should not get closer to the USSR. This is the wrong time to leave our friends.' (Mr Bhutto had made no suggestion that we 'leave our friends'.)

The then Foreign Secretary's conclusions which carried the implicit approval of the then Foreign Minister (who himself gave no views) *inter alia* were:

(a) 'At the present juncture we have no alternative but to remain friendly with the West. Having fortuitously become the strongest non-European power allied to the West, we should take advantage of the situation by not only showing but giving positive proof of our steadfastness and dependability.'

(b) 'We would have been faced with a very difficult choice: annoyance of China or annoyance of US . . . We have had to choose between the two and the force of circumstances demanded that we backed the US.' (The Foreign Secretary referred to the possibility of the US quitting the UN in the event of Peking's admission.)

(c) 'It is fashionable to criticise imperialism . . . I fear they (African countries under Portuguese colonialism) would have to face the problems of government and administration and I trust they, like Congo, would not become a UN responsibility involving all of us in a tremendous amount of expense . . . But we are now asked to vote against Portugal because the Afro-Asian opinion desires it . . . Is making of our vote available for every Afro-Asian enterprise in the UN the only method to win the support of the new nations? There are other methods also of cultivating public opinion which we are not using.'

(d) To extend our contacts and win influence at the United Nations 'would require a vision, a large heart and a larger purse. Since we have not got any of these (if I may say so respectfully though cynically), we should "lump" certain situations.'

These views were in accord with the prevailing thinking at the time. However, when Mr Z. A. Bhutto's views as well as the contrary opinions were considered at a special Cabinet Meeting on 18 November 1960, some of the decisions reached were as follows:

(a) 'It is true that they (the USA) have not found it possible for their own reasons to give us political support in our dispute with India. We understand their difficulty but then, because of that very reason, we have to fend for ourselves in this field . . . This, in turn, means that we should not adopt rigid postures towards Russia or China . . .'

(b) 'We should explain with conviction (to the United States) that in the present situation we have come to the conclusion that we should vote for the admission of the People's Republic of China at the next session . . .'

(c) 'The Government could not isolate itself by disregarding the public feeling as well as the feelings of all the Afro-Asian countries.'

Mr Z. A. Bhutto, Minister for Fuel, Power and Natural Resources, is likely to visit Moscow by the end of this month or early next month to finalise a credit agreement with the Soviet Union providing for technical assistance for oil exploration in Pakistan.

The Minister told this to pressmen on his arrival in Karachi from Lahore by PIA.

The Minister stated that the draft agreement, which is expected to arrive from the Soviet Union soon, will first be discussed by the Cabinet before he leaves for Moscow.

He further added the amount of credit Pakistan accepts from Russia will depend on the terms and conditions on which they are offered.

Mr Bhutto said he would conduct further negotiations in Moscow on the basis of the draft agreement submitted by Russia . . .

Mr Bhutto told a questioner that the supply of Sui Gas to India will depend on what terms the Indians will be willing to offer. He said gas was a very valuable item and only if attractive offers were made, would Pakistan supply it to India.

Moreover, he said no concrete proposal was made by the Indians after the talks on the subject between Prime Minister Nehru and President Ayub Khan during the former's visit to Pakistan.

Mr Bhutto will fly to Rawalpindi this evening and return to Karachi on November 9. – APP

Dawn, 8 November 1960

Excerpts from Memorandum addressed by Mr Z. A. Bhutto, Foreign Minister, on 11 May 1966 from Dacca to President Ayub Khan through Foreign Secretary.

Pakistan has its established links with the West. It is on terms of friendship and trust with China. Pakistan does not have a resident mission in Hanoi, but there have been sufficient contacts between Rawalpindi and Hanoi for it to be said that the relations between the two countries are friendly. Pakistan is in the most advantageous position to be approached in the search for a constructive initiative. Until recently, the United States completely ignored the most obvious country in its many efforts throughout the world to find an initiator for its high purpose. Apparently, the United States believed that if it approached Pakistan, it would be interpreted by that country as a glorious vindication of its China policy and thus encourage it to get even closer to China. However, basically the fear of this possibility is much less dangerous to the United States interests than its future in Vietnam. It was, therefore, inevitable that sooner or later the United States would approach Pakistan. This was done on the 20th of April, 1966, at Ankara when Secretary of State Rusk, almost pathetically appealed to me to do something about Vietnam. On two separate occasions in the same evening he said, 'Can you not arrange a meeting between me and Chen Yi in Geneva or Monaco or anywhere he wants? There should be no difficulty for you to visit Hanoi or Peking for this purpose.' I said to him that so far the United States had not taken Pakistan into confidence. Many preliminaries were involved and we were not prepared for such a mission. I informed him that I would get in touch with my Government and contact him on the following day. I immediately sent a telegram to the President in which I conveyed Mr Rusk's request and sought his instructions. On the 21st afternoon, Additional Foreign Secretary contacted Pakistan's Ambassador in Peking on the telephone and said that as the positions of the two parties were far apart, no reconciliation seemed possible. *Pakistan would not like to meddle in the affair and burn its fingers* (italics supplied). He went on to say that the President was, however, agreeable to sound the Chinese through their Ambassador in Pakistan on Rusk's request for a meeting with Chen Yi. Additional Foreign Secretary also informed Pakistan's Ambassador that in the President's view we should not give an impression to the Americans that we had influence on the Chinese. These telephonic instructions were confirmed by a subsequent telegram from Additional Foreign Secretary in which he repeated the gist of his conversation with Pakistan's Ambassador in Peking. When I met Mr Rusk on the evening of 21st, the Secretary of State said that he would like to keep in close touch with me on this question, but he resiled from his specific request and did not manifest the anxiety of the previous evening. It is possible that he changed his mind because the messages between Ankara and Rawalpindi were intercepted or for some other important reason. As the response from Rawalpindi was negative, I did not consider it advisable to probe him any further. The instructions that came from Rawalpindi were unhappily couched . . .

Before leaving Ankara for Washington, Secretary of State, Mr Rusk said on April 22nd that he had 'a two-hour talk on South-East Asia with Pakistan Foreign Minister, Mr Z. A. Bhutto', and that, they had exchanged views 'on the matter of contacts with China'. It is repeated that essentially Pakistan is most appropriately placed to seek ways of tackling the Vietnam question. Pakistan is in the best position to open communications between China and the United

States and Hanoi through China. Pakistan is an Asian country and a neighbour of China. It has developed special relationship with China without breaking its links with the West. It has forged friendly contacts with Hanoi. Even if its efforts failed it would not injure the interests of Pakistan. On the contrary, it would enhance Pakistan's prestige and show to the world that Pakistan alone is able to move substantially and more progressively in the right direction. It would show that Pakistan has constructive channels of communications with the United States and with China and has been able to maintain the confidence of both antagonists at war.

As the question is so important to peace in Asia and to the world at large, now is the time for Pakistan to play its part. We should not hesitate only because there is a risk of failure. Even if the efforts do fail they may bring the situation closer to the cherished realisation.

There are many indications to demonstrate that the situation is ripe for a meaningful initiative by an Asian State having good relations both with Peking and Hanoi and with Washington. In the present vortex of international affairs, it seems that it is Pakistan that happens to be that State. The gauntlet should be thrown. It may not succeed, but it will do no harm. It would establish our bonafides with both sides.

Zulfikar Ali Bhutto
11 May 1966, Camp Dacca

Excerpts from official memoranda by Mr Z̧. A. Bhutto, Foreign Minister – 1966.

(1)

Pakistan has so far chosen to ignore the powerful reality called the Soviet Union protruding on to its head. Indeed, it pursued a policy of belligerence towards that colossal power . . . It refused to have contact with the Soviet Union, and, on occasions, provided dangerous provocations to that country as, for instance, by allowing U-2 to take off from its territory to conduct espionage into the Soviet Union. Pakistan allowed the United States permanent facilities to pry on the Soviet Union. In the further pursuance of this one-dimensional foreign policy, Pakistan did not even feel the necessity of having any substantial cultural and commercial contacts with the Soviet Union. Soviet literature, even of a technical nature, was prevented from being disseminated. Whilst the world had gradually changed and the Soviet Union and the United States made their respective adjustments to the changes, Pakistan stood firm and refused to recognise the evolution of the times. It was not the responsibility of the United States to educate Pakistan on the changes that had taken place. It did no injury to the United States' interests to allow Pakistan to remain as firmly entrenched to the USA as it was before the changes. Also during the 1965 India-Pakistan war, when Western countries imposed an embargo on the shipment of military equipment both to India and Pakistan, the Indian leaders paid rich tributes to the Soviet Union for not having imposed a similar embargo on India and for continuing to supply India with military equipment according to the agreements reached between the Soviet Union and India before the hostilities began. During the war, with a smiling Mr Dean Rusk standing by his side, the Soviet Foreign Minister, Mr Gromyko said in New York, 'the Soviet Union was India's staunchest friend'. At the time of the critical Security Council debates leading to the September 20th Resolution, in each and every step, the Soviet Union supported India.

We seek to have good relations wih the United States because it is a great power and an influential country – a country with whom it is necessary to have good relations. Our relations with the United States are not based on any particular initiative taken by the United States, be they bilaterial or multilateral. It is on the basis of the strength and position of the United States as a great power. So also, we have good relations with China not because China gave an ultimatum to India during the September war. Our good relations with China preceded the ultimatum. Our relations with China have developed not on account of any particular initiative taken by China, but on account of the hard realities of geography, history and politics. If good relations with the great powers depend on each and every initiative either in favour or otherwise then there would be no continuity or certainty in State relations and no logical rules determining the course of relationship between the States. Therefore, it is essential for us to improve our relations with the Soviet Union independent of any particular initiative . . . This will give our relations a broader scope and much greater manoeuvreability.

It is necessary and vital for us to improve our relations with the Soviet Union. This should be done independent of any important initiative taken by the Soviet Union rather than in the confined context of any particular initiative.

Zulfikar Ali Bhutto
11 April 1966

(2)

The President is aware that for some time past I have argued the merits of developing bilaterial relations with foreign countries as against multilateral obligations so as to provide our foreign policy with latitude and logic.

For over twenty years the international situation was dominated by multilateral commitments. Now the situation is changing again. New factors have arisen and the prevailing conditions call for a return to an increasing emphasis on bilateral diplomacy.

Apart from the danger of multilateral conflicts, a State committed to a multilateral defence arrangement which does not strictly coincide with its own national interests suffers from a multitude of handicaps. Among the many vices of such multilateral arrangements is that the train is so composed as to move at the pace of the slowest and the result is conflict of interests and ineffectiveness in the face of specific exigencies. Simultaneously, inherent in this situation is the contradiction of the other extreme in which a State may want to proceed so fast as to cause the derailment of all the wagons in the train. In other words, it is difficult to move perennially on the basis of a rhythm which is in accord with the aspirations of each and every State within a multilateral undertaking.

Even bilateral relations can assume the character of a multilateral obligation if the terms of the bilateral relationship in essence assume multilateral commitments under a connected arrangement. For example, if a State were to give a commitment to one of the Great Powers to go to war if that Great Power were to be involved in war, it would in fact assume a multilateral obligation. This would be so because the Great Power concerned may have similar bilateral and multilateral obligations with other States. Thus, a chain reaction would ensue and bilateral commitments would be transformed into a multilateral obligation. Even a purely bilateral agreement could restrict the freedom of action of the participants if the nature of the agreement is such that it militates against the security of another State. For example, in such circumstances it would place the participants in a position from which they would find themselves severely restricted in the development of their bilateral relations with the third country against whose vital interests they have already concluded a bilateral agreement.

An essential pre-requisite of consistent and clean bilateral relations is the substance of non-alignment. The relations should be confined to the limits of common national interests of the two powers concerned and not commit themselves beyond the respective interests of the two powers which would be inimical to the interests of a third country.

Zulfikar Ali Bhutto
30 May 1966

(3)

Since the end of the Second World War a new political situation has arisen in the world which, perhaps because it is so obvious, is sometimes not seen in its correct perspective and its implications on the conduct of human affairs are not sufficiently understood . . .

The traditional method of conducting foreign affairs of a country in the 19th and the first half of the 20th century was to have regional alliance to maintain a balance of power among the grouping of the Great Powers with the assistance of the smaller nations. It was by maintaining a very delicate balance of power that peace was maintained; in fact, peace was disturbed only when the balance of power at any given time tilted in favour of one or the other group. In those days, smaller nations could influence the policy and the alignment of the Great Powers by indulging in various political permutations and combinations.

All this has changed today with the emergence of global powers which, in addition to having all the attributes of Great Powers in the classical sense, are at the same time bigger, much more powerful and play a much larger role in determining the destinies of the people all over the world. The emergence of these powers has radically changed the whole concept of conducting human affairs and affairs of State in the last twenty years. The task of the smaller nations, in which category all the developing nations fall, in determining their relationship with the Great Powers and in the furtherance of their national interests has been more complex and more difficult. The small nation which does not understand the new rules is doomed to frustration, a sense of helplessness, isolation and, perhaps, eventual extinction. We must fully understand how in this new situation we should conduct our own affairs.

The question before the smaller nations today is how to conduct their affairs in such a manner that their basic interests are safeguarded, they retain their territorial integrity and continue to have independence in their relationship with the Great Powers as well as with the smaller nations. It is obvious that it is not possible to attain equality among unequal forces. In such a situation the most one can expect is a relationship of tolerance, perhaps understanding, but never genuine equality. The relationship between the Great Powers and the smaller countries are *ipso facto* unequal in which the Great Powers can wrench out a multitude of advantages without responding in sufficient, leave alone equal, measure. It is not conceivable for a weaker nation to convert or seduce a Great Power to its point of view or to bring it under its influence on the noble plea of justice or the righteousness of its cause. In the ultimate analysis, it is not the virtue of the cause that becomes the determining factor but the cold global interests of Great Powers which determine their policy. These interests are bound to prevail in any open and endless confrontation among such unequal forces.

Does this mean that the smaller nations should obediently follow the dictates of Great Powers and exchange their independence for material gains and promise of economic prosperity? The answer is a resounding 'No'. It is possible with adroit handling of their affairs for the smaller nations to maintain their independence and have a flexibility of action in their relationship with Great Powers as well as smaller nations. It would be inexpedient and perhaps dangerous for a smaller nation to completely identify itself with the total interests of one Great Power to the exclusion of the others. Sometimes it might be necessary for a smaller nation to be more closely associated with one global power but, even so, it is not impossible for it to maintain normal relations with the others on the basis of honourable bilateral relations. It would be the quintessence of folly for a small State to pursue a policy of provocation towards any global power on the strength of support from another Great Power, or for any other pressing reason . . .

It would be idealistic to expect a Great Power to change its global objectives on the demand of a smaller State. It would be unrealistic for a weaker State to expect to convert a Great Power to its point of view before agreeing to have normal relations with it. As the relationship is unequal, it would be sagacious for a smaller State to isolate and set aside the point of conflict on the clear and categorical understanding that neither party will influence the other on that specific issue. On such a tacit understanding, a normal and logical association can be built. Such an understanding certainly does not mean that it should not have better relations with those Great Powers which support its point of view. Such an understanding brings about a gradation of relationships which are explicable, consistent and logical and free from misinterpretations. It does not mean that there is any loss of prestige or loss of face. On the contrary, it means that the smaller power is not willing to compromise its prestige, interests and position. It only means that there is an agreement on the part of both not to interfere or influence each other's position on a point on which there is a basic difference. It means that a *quid pro quo* is not being extracted for the establishment of normal relations. It only divorces a particular issue from direct dealings. It only avoids an unequal confrontation on condition that neither will influence each other on the vital point of disagreement. Such an understanding does not stop the State concerned from pursuing its struggle. Nor does it prevent a lively dialogue on the differences whenever suitable opportunities arise . . .

The simple fact of the matter is that in the long run, a Great Power cannot be out-witted or out-smarted. It would thus be better to take a realistic and balanced attitude and evolve a policy on scientific rather than on subjective lines.

The objectives of the State concerned would stand better chances of being realized by other means – by the application of indirect pressures exerted by the collective voice and solidarity of the smaller nations of Asia, Africa and Latin America, whom we now call the Third World together with diplomatic pressure from the Great Powers and the marginal Great Powers with whom its interest coincide. The principal tactic should be to dodge a direct confrontation with the Great Powers with whom basic interests are at variance . . .

It is, therefore, necessary for smaller States to maintain a dialogue on their conflicting interests with all Great Powers irrespective of their positions, to do all within their resources to influence them indirectly without getting entangled on a narrow one-dimension basis of all or nothing.

With the point of conflict set aside, there can be normal and friendly dealings with all Great Powers in question on all matters except on the issue of conflict. This would enable the State in question to have the latitude for more cordial relations with those Great Powers with whom its interests coincide. In such an event, the Great

Power whose interests clash, cannot take exception to that State's more cordial relations with the Great Powers with whom its interests coincide . . .

Solidarity of the Third World is so important to the less powerful nations that the Great Powers do not derive any special comfort from the emergence of this phenomenon. At present, this solidarity is not strong enough to be asserted as an effective lever against the Great Powers . . .

It would be clearly understood that the whole basis of our foreign policy is to consolidate relations with those who support us and insulate the points of conflict with those that are either neutral or opposed to us . . .

Therefore, it is in the fitness of the dynamics and dignity of the world situation that smaller powers should seek to isolate the areas of conflict in the pursuit of their national objectives and not come to a head-on collision with the Great Powers with the vagaries and vicissitudes of their changing objectives . . .

The theory of causation is as much applicable to foreign affairs as it is to the law of tort. There is an active inter-relationship and mutual influence in the conduct of State relations. A clean and praise-worthy foreign policy influences other States. Correspondingly, an expedient or unscrupulous policy adversely affects the image of a State in its relations with other countries. If Pakistan's policies remain consistent and moral and are of a lofty tone and character, other States are bound to be influenced by such an attitude and behaviour . . .

It is thus feasible and indeed desirable for Pakistan to maintain bilateral relations with both the Great and the quasi-Great Powers on a perfectly understandable gradation, but without any strain and tension. Bilateral relations, in order to be productive need to be consistent and not at the cost of relations with other countries . . . The terms of bilateral relations should not in any way be inconsistent or cut across the ambit and scope of the bilateral relations with the other Great States.

Zulfikar Ali Bhutto
15 April 1966

The article on Bilateralism contains references which have been clarified by reproducing the relevant excerpts from Government documents. Their publication was formally authorized by the Government Departments concerned and the correspondence relating to authorization duly published.

INDEX

INDEX

Abraham   81
Afghanistan   77
Africa   32
    countries of   23, 24, 26, 27, 28, 36, 37, 38, 41,
        86, 89, 129; disunity between   66
    famine in   20
Aid-to-Pakistan Consortium   49
Al-Aqsa Mosque, Jerusalem   77
Al-Quds, *see* Jerusalem
Algeria   87
Algiers   18
Algiers Charter   18
Ali Khan, Ghazanfar   107
Ali Khan, Liaquat   107
Ali, Salman Ahmad   110
Angola   66
Ankara   49
Arab-Israeli War (1973)   74, 77, 79–80, 85
Arab-Jewish conflict, causes of   78
    see also Arab-Israeli war; Palestine
Arab League   18

Arab unity, need for   65
    present lack of   66
Arab world   32
Asia, countries of   23, 24, 26, 27, 28, 36, 37, 38,
    39, 41, 86, 89, 129
Ayub Khan   49, 50, 108
    presidentship of   43
    correspondence of author with   44–6, 112–14
    quoted   110, 111, 115

Bada Ber surveillance base   43
Bandaranaike, Sirimavo   19
Bandung   26
Bandung Conference   26–7, 37, 53
Bangladesh   97
    recognized by Pakistan   77
Bhutto, Zulfikar Ali   16, 30, 60, 74, 94, 108, 109
    resigns as Foreign Minister   50–51
    texts of correspondence and memoranda
        112–15, 117–30
Bilateralism:
    definitions of   31–3, 50
    as feature of post-Second World War world
        34–6
    necessity of for developing nations   51–2, 58
    and relationships with great powers   51–5, 97
    notes   103–30
    see also non-alignment
British Empire   34
British Mandate in Palestine   76

Cairo   18
Canada   57, 58

CENTO 69
  shortcomings of organization 67–8
Chen Yi 123
Chiang Kai-Shek 105, 106, 119
China, People's Republic of 35, 40, 41–2, 51, 65
  representation in United Nations 41–2, 46–7,
    105–6, 108, 117, 118–19, 120
  relations with Pakistan 41–2, 45, 47, 48–9,
    50, 95–6, 110–11, 123–4, 125
  see also Sino-Indian conflict
Chou En-lai 42, 50, 95
Cold War 34, 35, 47, 63
Colombo 18, 26, 71, 72
Colombo Conference 19, 26
colonialism, Western 78, 84
  residual 32
  twilight of 34
  dismantling of 35, 51, 76
  experience of 38
  aftermath to 100
  see also neo-colonialism
Common Market, *see* European Economic Community
  munity
Congressional Record-House 110
Crusades 81

Dakar decisions 18
Dawn (Karachi) 107, 110, 112, 115, 122
Declaration on World Peace and Cooperation 53
Delhi 47
Denmark 47
détente, policy of between great powers 51
  implications of 63–4, 96–7
developed countries 26–7, 85
  economic power of 20–22, 23–4, 27
  see also developing countries

developing countries   19, 26
    need for unity among   20, 21, 24–8, 86, 91
    disadvantaged position of   20–21, 22–4, 84–5,
        86
    relationships with great powers   34–7
    see also Bilateralism; non-alignment; Third
        World
dialogue, need for between rich and poor nations
        17, 24, 129

East Asia   165–6
East Europe   64
East Pakistan   97
    civil war in   50
    Indian invasion of   50
    see also Bangladesh
economy, international, imbalanced nature of   22
    case for redistribution of power in   25–6
Egypt   37, 65
Europe   51
    see also East Europe; West Europe
European Economic Community (EEC)   24, 99

First World War   62
Formosa, *see* Taiwan
France   34, 57

Gandhi, Indira   101
Geneva   80

Georgetown   18
Germany   34
   Federal Republic of   57
Golan Heights   80
great powers, the, emergence of   33–4
   and pressures on developing countries   34–6,
     38–9, 58, 87, 108, 126–7
   relations with Pakistan   40–44, 23–30
   and question of Bilateralism   51–5, 128–30
   see also détente; U.S.A.; U.S.S.R.
Gromyko, A.A.   125
Group of Non-Aligned Countries   19, 71
   Summit Conference of   16, 26
Group of Seventy Seven   16, 18, 25
Gunderson, Oakar   110

Hanoi   122, 124
Helsinki Conference   64, 96
Hutchinson, George   94
   interview with author   95–103

IAEA   57
India:
   initiates policy of non-alignment   37
   disputes with Pakistan   37, 41, 44, 45–6, 50;
     and need for reconciliation   101–2
   nuclear programme of   58
   see also Sino-Indian dispute
Indo-Soviet Treaty (1971)   50
Indonesia   77, 84
intercontinental ballistic missiles   54

International Civil Aviation Organization 101
International Development Association 24
international institutions, shortcoming of 23–4
   see also United Nations
Iqbal, Muhammad 75, 76, 84
Iran 32, 76, 99
   and RCD 60, 61, 62, 66, 67, 69
   see also Regional Cooperation for Development
Islamic Conference 18, 32, 100
   First Summit, at Rabat 77
   Second Summit, at Lahore 74; author's
     address to 75–92
   Charter of 83
Islamic world:
   culture of 40
   Pakistan's position in 42–3, 76–7
   see also Muslim states
Israel:
   nuclear programme of 58, 65
   occupation of Palestine 79
   attitude of nationalist aggression 79–80, 81
   occupation of Jerusalem 81–3
   see also Arab-Israeli War; Zionism
Izmir Conference 60
   author's address on eve of 61–73

Jammu 44, 45, 46, 57, 101, 113, 114, 116
   see also Kashmir
Japan 34, 51, 66
Jerusalem 74, 77, 78, 80
   key role in Palestine question 81–2, 91
Jesus 81
Jinnah, Quaid-i-Azam Mohammed Ali, founder
   of Pakistan 41, 75, 76
Johnson, Lyndon B. 48, 49

Karachi   42, 47, 107
Kashmir:
    Pakistan-India dispute over   41, 44, 45–6,
        57, 101, 102, 108, 109, 112–14, 115, 116
Khrushchev, Nikita S.   43, 109–10
Kissinger, Henry   48, 49, 50, 69
Korean War   43, 105

Ladakh:
    Sino-Indian dispute over   44–6,   112–14,
        115–16
Lahore   60, 74, 75–6
Laos conflict   43
Latin America, countries of   18, 23, 24, 26, 27,
        28, 37, 39, 41, 89, 129
    régimes in   66
Lebanon   65
Leninist-socialism   35
Lima Declaration and Action Programme   18

Maghreb   84
Malaysia   77
Manila Declaration   18
Mao Tse-tung   95
Menon, Krishna   114
Mexico Conference   16, 26
    author's paper written on eve of   17–28
Middle East   40, 70, 76, 78, 91
    as continuing crisis area   65, 79
    conditions for settlement in   80–81
Morning News (Karachi)   111, 112, 116
Moses   81

Muslim-Jewish relations 78
Muslim League 76
Muslim states:
    need for unity between 73, 78, 86–90
    and the Palestine question 79–83
    in the colonial and post-colonial eras 84–5
    future role of 86–7, 88–9

National Assembly Debate 108
nationalism:
    reassertions of 51
    larger Muslim 73, 89–90
NATO 64, 65, 69
Near East 70
Nehru, Jawaharlal 37, 111, 115, 116
neo-colonialism 19
non-aligned countries 18, 19
    see also Group of Non-Aligned Countries
non-alignment, meaning of 16, 25–6
    as necessary policy 36–40
    see also Bilateralism
Norway 47, 109
nuclear technology:
    misapprehensions over Pakistan's need for 57–8

oil, importance of as trade commodity 20
oil crisis, effects of 21
oil-producing countries 20, 50, 85, 99
    and division within Third World 86
Organization of African Unity (OAU) 18

Pahlavi, H.I.M. Mohammed Reza, Shahanshah
    of Iran 67
Pakistan 23, 87
    call for Third World Summit 26
    policy of Bilateralism 31–2, 58–9
    disputes with India 37, 41, 44, 45–6; and
        need for reconciliation 101–2
    relations with U.S.A. 40, 41, 43–4, 48–50, 98
    relations with People's Republic of China
        41–2, 45, 47, 48–9, 50, 105–6, 118–19, 123–4
    relations with U.S.S.R. 42, 47–8, 50, 124–7
    errors of previous leadership in 43–4, 47, 49,
        97
    justification for nuclear programme 57–8
    and RCD 60, 61, 62, 66, 67, 69
    relations with West 97–9
    future progress in 103
Pakistan-India War (1965) 48, 49, 125
Palestine:
    objections to partition of 43, 57, 76, 79, 83,
        91
    root causes of problem 78–9
Paris Conference 16, 24, 99
Peking 49, 50
Persian Gulf 99
Peshawar 43
Portugal 34
Pyongyang 16

Qadir, Manzur 108
    author's correspondence with 45, 46–7, 115,
        118–19
Quran, the Holy 81
    quoted 88, 92

Rabat 77
Rawalpindi 50
Regional Cooperation for Development (RCD) 60, 67
  conferences of 60
  present shortcomings of 68
  future of 69–70
  Charter of 72
rich and poor nations, and widening divisions between 16, 17, 20, 21, 22, 23
  see also developing nations; Third World
Rusk, Dean 49, 123, 125
Russia, Tsarist 34
Russia, Soviet, *see* U.S.S.R.

Sahara 65
Saudi Arabia 32
SEATO 69, 105
Second World War 33, 34, 62, 84
Simla Agreement (1972) 101
Sinai 80
Sino-Indian conflict 37, 44, 45–6, 48, 49, 112–14
Socialist bloc, countries of 51
South Africa:
  nuclear ambitions of 58, 66
Spain 34
Spectator 94
  interview with author from 95–103
Sri Lanka 19
Suez Canal, crisis 43, 107–8
Suhrawardy, H. S.:
  quoted 107–8
super powers, *see* great powers

Taiwan 42, 106–7
Tashkent Declaration 49, 50
Teheran 61
Third World:
    countries of 20, 21, 22, 32, 129
    need to promote unity between 18, 19, 24–8,
        88–9, 91
    need for development in 22–3
    path to economic independence in 25–6,
        85–7
    nationalism in 51
Third World Summit:
    call for, and terms of reference of 16, 26–8,
        39–40
Tibet 44
Times, The 94
Times of India 111
Tito (Joseph Broz) 38
Trade and Development Organization 25
Turkey 32, 76
    and RCD 60, 61, 62, 66, 67, 69
    see also Regional Cooperation for Development

U-2 spy-plane affair 43, 124
UNCIP resolution 113
UNCTAD:
    Fourth Congress 99
United Nations 18, 32, 35, 37, 51, 76, 87, 101
    Development Programme 24
    Charter 32, 35, 53, 56, 72, 81, 98
    representation of People's Republic of China
       in 41–2, 46–7, 105–6, 108, 117, 118–19,
       120
    and Kashmir dispute 45, 46
    'powerlessness' of 56–7
    and Palestine question 79

United Nations General Assembly   26, 38, 44
    Sixth Special Session   16, 18
    Seventh Special Session   18
    Fifteenth Session   120
United Nations Security Council   114
    Resolution   242, 81
U.S.A.   33, 51, 57, 58, 105
    relations with Pakistan   40, 41, 43–4, 48–50,
    98, 122–4, 125
    see also détente; great powers
U.S. Congress   98
U.S.S.R.   33, 37, 40, 51, 64
    relations with Pakistan   42, 47–8, 50, 97,
    124–7
    see also détente; great powers

Vietnam   122–3
    East Asia after war in   65–6

West Europe:
    culture and civilization of   35, 62, 90
    future potential of   70–71
    see also colonialism; European Economic
    Community

Yayah Khan:
    régime of   49

Zafrullah Khan, Chaundhri Mohammed   107
Zionism, condemnation of   78